SARDINIA

Jack Altman

J·P·M
PUBLICATIONS

CONTENTS

This Way Sardinia	**3**
Map: Sardinia	6–7
Flashback	**8**
On the Scene	**15**
Cagliari	*16*
The Port 17, The Citadel 17, About Town 18	
The South	*21*
Iglesiente 21, Sarrabus 23	
The West	*25*
Oristano 25, Tharros 28, Arborea 28, Barumini 29, Nuraghe Losa 30, Bosa 30	
Northwest	*32*
Alghero 32, Sassari 35, Romanesque Churches 37, Torralba 38, Porto Torres 38, Castelsardo 39, Perfugas 39	
Northeast	*40*
Olbia 40, Posada 40, Costa Smeralda 41, North Coast Resorts 42, Maddalena Islands 44, Gallura 46	
Map: The Northeast	43
The Centre	*47*
Nuoro 47, Oliena 50, Barbagia 51, The Coast 53	
Cultural Notes	**54**
Shopping	**56**
Dining Out	**57**
Sports	**59**
The Hard Facts	**60**
Index	65

This Way Sardinia

Wild Beauty

In the language of gemstones commonly used to describe islands and shorelines, Costa Smeralda—Emerald Coast—is a natural name for Sardinia's renowned resort development looking out over the limpid green waters of the northeast shore. By the same token, the island itself gives the impression of a splendid rough diamond. Sardinia has its share of fine beaches, romantic coves and lively port cities, but its special treasure is the rugged beauty of the unspoiled landscapes of the interior.

With their own craggy simplicity, the people match the terrain. Like many other Mediterranean islanders, their disposition is not quite as sunny as the climate. In face of the annual arrival of foreign visitors—regarded as the latest, though perhaps friendliest wave in centuries of invasions—Sardinians display a hospitable, if cool and dignified, reserve.

Sardinia is very much a land apart from the rest of Italy. Unlike the other Italian islands of Sicily, Capri, Ischia or Elba, it stands aloof from the mainland. Its real neighbour is Corsica, whose white chalk cliffs are visible 12 km (7 miles) to the north across the Strait of Bonifacio.

With most of the 1,700,000 people living along the coast, the inland region remains sparsely populated. Sardinia's land surface of 24,090 sq km (9,300 sq miles) makes it the Mediterranean's second-largest island, after Sicily. It is made up almost entirely of one hilly plateau split only in the southwest corner by the Campidano lowland extending from Oristano down to Cagliari. The highest peak, La Marmora in the central Monti del Gennargentu, is just 1,834 m (6,017 ft) above sea level. But ravines, crags, valleys and steep, densely wooded hillsides make the island look more mountainous than it really is. Each rural community lives very separately from the other, a historical obstacle to "national" unity. The Romans despised the perennially rebellious interior as "barbarian", a name that has stuck to it in modern Italian as Barbagia.

The rich Campidano farmland, once an important "granary" for the Roman Empire, grows wheat, barley, grapes and olives, as well as tobacco. The vast tracts of cork

3

This Way Sardinia

Sardinia's greatest asset is its coastline, with crystal-clear waters, craggy cliffs and spectacular views.

oak make Sardinia Italy's largest supplier of cork. The uplands are sheep and goat country. The small, tough Sardinian sheep number almost 4 million, more than a third of Italy's total. Since the 1890s, the ewes produce milk for the much coveted tangy *pecorino* cheese. Fisheries bring in good catches of tuna, mullet, spiny lobster, eel and, of course, sardines. Until recent years, they have been strictly for export, since seafood was never a staple of the Sardinians' own cuisine. The tastes of foreign visitors at the resorts have changed this, but the great local specialities remain roast pig, lamb or goat.

Stone Sentinels

The island cannot boast of much grand architecture, but it has an astounding array of unique prehistoric monuments, the towering stone *nuraghi*. Archaeologists date the oldest back at least to 1600 BC and have located the remains of over 7,000 scattered across the island. The most impressive are Su Nuraxi at Barumini, north of Cagliari, and in the Valley of Nuraghi near Torralba, east of Alghero. Preceding the invasions of Phoenicians, Romans, Arabs, Catalans and Italians, they are regarded as stone guardians of the one golden era when Sardinia was independent.

Coastal counterparts to the *nuraghi*, massive watchtowers were built at almost every port or harbour over the centuries to fend off the perennial threat of pirates. Apart from a couple of amphitheatres and public baths, the Romans mainly left their mark with a remarkable network of roads. The original paving is often still visible, and their routes have largely been preserved for the excellent modern highways crisscrossing the island. The finest of the island's churches are Romanesque in the Pisan or Lombard style, with some handsome Catalan Gothic or Baroque edifices.

Sardinia's eye-catching modern art form is a series of colourful mural paintings, mostly in rural villages. They usually deal with social themes promoting Sardinian autonomy, folklore or the environment.

Shepherds and Bandits

In the old days, Sardinian townspeople and farmers in a charitable mood liked to define bandits as shepherds who had lost their flocks. When they were feeling particularly mean, they would describe a shepherd as a bandit with sheep. Today, the island's time-honoured banditry—Roman geographer Strabo was already complaining about it back in the 1st century BC—has to all intents and purposes disappeared. After a brief resurgence following World War II, theft and other crimes are now considerably lower than the national average.

Shepherds, on the other hand, are still going strong. Whether townspeople and farmers like it or not, they remain the standard-bearers of the island's indomitable spirit. Tough, dour and proud, many of them have firmly resisted attempts made by Italian mainlanders to modernize their sheep-rearing with larger herds for cooperative wool, meat and cheese production. As soon as your eyes meet their clear, piercing gaze, you are easily persuaded that this is a people of character.

THE BEST BOULDER Sardinia is famous for its weirdly shaped rocks, sculpted by thousands of years of wind and rain: vultures, elephants, even a head that looks just like Mussolini. Our favourite is the menacing bear at **Capo d'Orso** near Palau on the northeast coast.

flashback

Cutting Edge of the Stone Age

Sardinia made its entrance on the world stage around 6000 BC by offering its European neighbours a fine range of axes, knives and razor blades. They were honed from slivers of top-quality translucent black obsidian hewn from the volcanic rock of Mount Arci (south of modern Oristano) and traded overseas in Tuscany, Provence and Catalonia.

But the first real signs of communal life are the warrens of burial chambers found scattered around the island. Cut from solid rock, square entrances lead deep underground to as many as 20 different family tombs linked by corridors, like Egyptian mausoleums in the Nile Valley. Some tombs (4000–3000 BC) are decorated with magic emblems, bull's horns and geometric symbols, together with buxom figures of fertility goddesses, ornaments and traces of food to accompany the deceased into the afterlife. The chambers, some domed like bread-ovens, some rectangular with ceilings carved to imitate wooden rafters, seem to reproduce on a smaller scale the ancient dwellings of the living. In fact, their design is not so very different from latterday rural abodes in the Barbagia hills. Sardinians have dubbed them *domus de janas*, "witches' homes".

Age of the Nuraghi

The first of the great stone towers that have become the island's landmarks were erected around 1600 BC. The root of their name, *nur*, means "hollowed mass of stone". As can be deduced from bronze or stone models found as votive offerings in tombs, their cone-shaped form was originally flattened at the top with battlements. They were surrounded by ramparts, smaller towers and bastions and clusters of circular village dwellings, though never attaining the size of a city. The towers' dry-stone construction made no use of mortar and rose to heights of 22 m (72 ft), often three storeys of rooms reached by a spiralling inner corridor.

Whether castle, temple, mausoleum or all three—archaeologists are not sure—they are an imposing architectural achievement. No other Mediterranean sculpture at this time can match the refinement of bronze deities, heroes and warriors found in vaulted burial chambers (now on display in Cagliari's archaeological museum).

Of the same era, and equally formidable for the prowess of their construction were the *tombe dei giganti*, Giants' Tombs. The tombs rather than the occupants were giant-sized, with finely carved monoliths, 4 m (13 ft) high, used for the entrance and walls of mausoleum mounds housing 100 or more individual graves in an enclosure stretching up to 30 m (98 ft) in length.

The Phoenicians

The first Phoenicians arrived around 1000 BC from Biblical Canaan and Lebanon. After the collapse of Crete's maritime empire, they had become the most enterprising traders of the ancient Mediterranean world. They moved westwards to settle along the coasts of North Africa and southern Spain, the Balearic Islands, Corsica, Sardinia and western Sicily. In Sardinia, they were interested in Monte Arci's obsidian, the copper, lead and silver mined in the southwest Iglesiente region, and the wheat of the Campidano lowland.

By the 6th century BC the Phoenicians had founded Sardinia's first cities: Kàralis (Cagliari); Tharros (near to modern Oristano); Sulcis (now Sant'Antioco); Nora, principal port for the Iglesiente mines; and Olbia in the northeast, peopling them with new settlers from their North African colony at Carthage. Garrison towns in the interior, notably Macomer, were established to put down sporadic revolts from the islanders.

The Phoenicians were also skilful artists. Excavations have revealed a rich panoply of bronze figures, jewellery, fine ceramics and perfume bottles. Scholars suggest that the dark passions of such Semitic deities as Astarte and Tanit have lived on in Sardinian folklore, most obviously in the masks and costumed dances of Carnival.

The Romans Take Over

To wrest control of the western Mediterranean from Carthage, Rome launched the first of the so-called Punic Wars (264–241 BC). "Punic" was the Romans' term for the Phoenician colonists and synonymous with treachery. But in Sardinia it was the Phoenicians who were betrayed, by a mutiny of the island's mercenaries. In 238 BC, the Romans breached their peace treaty with Carthage by invading Sardinia (and Corsica). This time the mercenaries sided with the Phoenicians in mountain guerrilla warfare.

The Romans emerged victorious, but they never completely conquered the interior, dismiss-

ing the inhabitants as *civitates Barbariae*, forerunners of the island's infamous bandits of the Barbagia. For Cicero, the great orator and lawyer who came to Olbia to defend the island's governor against corruption charges in 54 BC, all Sardinians were trouble-makers, "nothing but descendants of despicable Carthaginians". He was also horrified by the malarial mosquitoes but recognized that, together with Sicily and North Africa, Sardinia was invaluable as one of the Roman Republic's three main granaries.

Until the empire collapsed in the 5th century AD, Sardinia served the Romans as an important bridgehead to their colonies in Spain and North Africa. They built a formidable network of roads, developed garrison towns with ancient *nuraghi* as fortifications, and greatly expanded lead and silver mining in the Iglesiente. Cagliari took over from Nora as the island's capital, and an important new northern port was built, *Turris Libisonis* (modern Porto Torres). Romanization also made the Sardinian dialect the most Latin of the empire's neo-Latin languages.

Sedilo's July horse race commemorates a victory of Emperor Constantine in 312.

Under Christian Rule

For some 500 years after the fall of the western empire, the Byzantine rulers in Constantinople kept Sardinia nominally as an imperial possession. Christianity came to the island as an eastern-style religion with Byzantine monasteries. Never sanctified by Rome, Emperor Constantine is still honoured as an island saint—Santu Antine—with an important sanctuary overlooking Lake Omodeo. Law courts and the bureaucracy were also organized along Byzantine lines. Figs and other eastern Mediterranean fruits were added to local agriculture.

From the 8th century, Arab raids forced coastal communities to flee to the interior. In 1016, Pope Benedict VIII persuaded Pisa and Genoa to send in troops to deliver Sardinia from control of the Arab prince, Mugahid el-Amiri. Rome sent in its monks to win over the hearts and minds of the peasantry by teaching Roman Catholic doctrine and liturgy and reorganizing the agriculture. Over the next 200 years, Tuscan and French architects, masons and sculptors arrived to build a total of 182 churches in the Pisan and Lombard Romanesque style—notably Santa Giusta at Oristano, Santissima Trinità di Saccargia near Sassari and Sant' Antioco di Bisarcio near Ozieri.

FLASHBACK

The Italians sought more security for their commercial activities by building fortified port cities at Alghero, Bosa and Castelgenovese (now Castelsardo), a new citadel for Cagliari, and the city of Sassari, safely inland and less vulnerable to the malarial coastal plain than Porto Torres. In the long run, the Pisan and Genoese merchants were too competitive to remain allies. Emperor Frederick Barbarossa tried to divide the island between the two, but both wanted it all. Local land-owners played off one side against the other in an endless series of battles and sieges.

In 1297, Pope Boniface VIII, claiming Sardinia as part of the heritage of his predecessor, St Peter, offered the island to the Catalans.

Catalan Occupation

For Jaime II, King of Aragon and Count of Barcelona (1260–1327), Sardinia was a welcome asset in his wars with the Arabs for control of the western Mediterranean. His son Alfonso defeated the recalcitrant Pisans at sea and occupied the island with an army of 10,000 men in 1323. The most serious resistance came in the Arborea province around Oristano, led by the judge Mariano and, after his death, by his courageous daughter Eleonora. As governing magistrate, she published the constitutional charter drawn up by her father, which remained in force for the island's rural interior from 1392 until the 19th century. The *Carta de Logu*, written in Sardinian dialect when all other official documents were drawn up in Catalan, Castilian Spanish and later Italian, became a rallying point for Sardinian autonomy.

This era was not a lot of fun for the islanders. High-handed in the cities, the Catalans divided the countryside into 376 fiefs under largely absentee landlords. Their greedy bailiffs took their own hefty share off the top of already oppressive taxes. Plague, bad harvests and famine in the 15th century reduced the population from 340,000 to 150,000. Impoverished herdsmen turned to banditry.

The rebellious Genoese citizens of Alghero, starved into submission by Pedro IV's siege in 1354, were banished and replaced by Catalans. They were allowed back in to work (as at Cagliari's Citadel) only during daylight hours. Alghero became known as Barceloneta and has remained to this day Catalan in dialect, architecture and popular traditions. Jewish merchants, scholars and doctors formed an important part of the Catalan colonies in Alghero and Cagliari until their expulsion in 1492. The Spanish Inquisition was introduced in the 16th century, aimed principally at blasphemy, bigamy and witchcraft.

The Jesuits founded universities at Sassari and Cagliari in the late 16th and early 17th centuries. In an atmosphere of deep religiosity, many churches were built in Catalan Gothic style and later Baroque, with a flourishing school of inspirational altar painting. But art in the style of the Italian Renaissance was discouraged as too independent-minded, with the artists of Sassari a notable exception. The most distinctive landmarks were the 66 coastal watchtowers built to guard against the constant threat of pirates.

Back to Italy

In 1720, diplomatic bargaining after the War of Spanish Succession left Sardinia in the reluctant hands of the Piedmontese House of Savoy. Absent-mindedly ruled from Turin, the island sank into anarchy, its countryside prey to bandits and inter-village vendettas. Count Giovanni Battista Bogino, minister of King Carlo Emanuele III, arrived in 1743 to reform banking and administration. He also reopened the universities and encouraged wayward shepherds to settle down as farmers.

But Vittorio Amedeo III dismissed the progressive count, and outside the major cities Sardinia resumed the feudal legacy of the Spanish. At the end of the 18th century, a few bourgeois intellectuals, shepherds and peasants developed revolutionary ideas of the Enlightenment, directed not at the monarchy but against the feudal land-owners. Their leader, magistrate Giovanni Maria Angioy, had to flee to Paris where he died in 1808, dreaming he could get the French to "liberate" Sardinia.

Agricultural closure laws were passed in the 1820s to end the feudal deadlock with new private enterprise farming. But the aristocrats exploited the laws to tighten their hold on lands and forests, restricting the shepherds' grazing rights and the peasants' access to arable land. Once again, banditry seemed to be the natural alternative.

In 1847, urban intellectuals and enlightened businessmen campaigned to tie Sardinia more closely to mainland Piedmont. Giuseppe Garibaldi, champion of national unity, set up home on the offshore isle of Caprera to reassure Sardinians of their common Italian destiny. But islanders remained suspicious when Roman businessmen arrived in the 1890s to modernize cheese production for the manufacture of the prized

FLASHBACK

pecorino. Although civic government buildings expressed bourgeois prosperity in Cagliari and Sassari, strikes and cost-of-living riots erupted among the new industrial proletariat.

20th Century

In World War I, Sardinia won national recognition and gratitude with the heroic battle victories of the Sassari Brigade, against overwhelming odds. Indeed, the island's 13,000 war victims represented 14 per cent of the mobilized force, much higher than the national average. The sacrifice encouraged Sardinian demands for more control of its own administration. The war veterans' *Movimento Combattentistico* grew into the Sardinian Action Party—*Partito Sardo d'Azione*—which ultimately led to the island's Regional Statute of Special Autonomy in 1948. With Cagliari as capital, this has divided the island into four provinces with Sassari, Oristano and Olbia as the other administrative capitals.

But first, Sardinia had to go through the arduous experience of fascism and another world war. The hysterically nationalistic Mussolini had no time for regional claims, but he did build the coal mining community of Carbonia and other new towns like Fertilia and Arborea. His fight against the island's chronic malaria was more ambitious than effective. A subsequent four-year Italo-American programme was successful, proudly recording 1950 as the first year in which no one died of the disease in Sardinia. An immediate consequence was the island's last invasion—the growth of tourism, most spectacularly with the Aga Khan's development of the Costa Smeralda resorts on the north coast.

Today, Sardinia continues its valiant balancing act between ancient traditions and the charms of modern prosperity.

---

2 THE TWO BEST MUSEUMS Many of the bigger towns have good museums devoted to the fine arts, folklore and the island's fascinating prehistory. At **Cagliari**, the Archaeology Museum in the Cittadella dei Musei is a splendid modern installation with exhibits well explained in English and Italian. The Folklore Museum in **Nuoro** gives you a perfect introduction to the island's traditional way of life.

On the Scene

Sardinia has first-rate highways for convenient day trips. To explore the south, the island-capital Cagliari is the obvious starting point for the rugged Iglesiente region and the beaches around Villasimius. Oristano makes a good base for west coast resorts and some of the most impressive of the island's prehistoric nuraghi. Further north, Alghero offers easy access to Castelsardo on the coast and busy Sassari inland. On the northeast corner, combine the Costa Smeralda resorts with the isles of Maddalena and Caprera. Start out from Nuoro for tours of the mountainous Barbagia interior.

CAGLIARI
The Port, The Citadel, About Town

The Sardinian capital is a bustling port city whose monuments trace the island's history from its ancient Phoenician and Roman beginnings to the modern day. The Phoenicians called it *Kàralis*, after the basalt rock on which its citadel was subsequently built. Merchants from their great colony of Carthage settled there in the 8th century BC; they appreciated the ideal sheltered position on the Golfo degli Angeli (Bay of Angels), one of the most beautiful natural harbours in the Mediterranean. After successively providing a maritime stronghold for Romans, Arabs, Pisans and Catalans, the town served as a submarine base in World War II and was heavily bombed by American planes in 1943.

Reconstruction and restoration have preserved a picturesque core of ancient, medieval and Baroque architecture, while modern additions sprawl across ten hills. Today, with a population of more than 230,000, the town is the seat of regional government, as well as a commercial port for its petrochemical refineries and for exporting the agricultural produce of the Campidano hinterland.

The Port

Start your visit of the town where the good people of Cagliari take their own ceremonial evening stroll, the *passeggiata*: under the arcades of Via Roma. The café terraces here offer fine vantage points for watching the parade of the local bourgeoisie and its golden youth, as well as the port traffic of tugs, fishing boats and international freighters. The ferries serve Genoa, Civitavecchia, Naples, Palermo and Tunis.

Palazzo Comunale

Facing the sea at the corner of the broad boulevard of Largo Carlo Felice, the dazzling white neo-Gothic-Catalan city hall, topped by twin, crenelled towers, was built at the end of the 19th century. Its design has been much criticized by modernists (and Italian nationalists), but more indulgent observers welcome this expansive gesture to the town's Catalan past and appreciate the dignity of the council chamber decorated with Italian and Flemish tapestries.

Opposite the city hall are the tourist information office and the bus station.

Behind the Port

In the crisscross of narrow streets between Via Roma and the Citadel, you will find some of the town's best traditional Sardinian restaurants—and a plethora of pizzerias. Cagliari's more elegant boutiques and jewellery shops are located on Via Manno and Via Sardegna.

The Citadel

Up on its elongated rock, the fortified Castello—*Casteddu* to Sardinians—stands at the historic heart of Cagliari. Defences were erected here by the merchants and soldiers of Pisa, who took over the Byzantine *Kastrum Kàralis* in 1217. The present walls are Piedmontese and Catalan extensions. They enclosed not only a fortress, but also the cathedral, churches, imposing palaces (the viceroy's palace is now the Prefettura), and residences for Catalan and Jewish merchants and bankers.

Around St Remy Bastion

The rampart was built in 1899 for Cagliari's citizens to enjoy the magnificent panorama over the town and the Golfo degli Angeli from its Terrazza Umberto I. The nearby 18th-century university buildings today house the library. Beyond it is the Pisans' famous Torre dell'Elefante (1307), with an elephant sculpted into the tower's gate on the seaward side. It was a popular place for viewing the heads of decapitated criminals. In the vicinity are two 17th-century Baroque churches,

San Giuseppe and Santa Croce. The latter was built by Jesuits from a synagogue that had been left to crumble after the Jews were expelled from the island.

Cattedrale di Santa Maria

The present characteristic Pisan Romanesque façade is a 20th-century reconstitution of the original. Built by the Pisans in the 13th century, the church was incomplete when the town was conquered by the Catalans, who finished it in Gothic style, later adding its Baroque interior. Inside, on either side of the western entrance, are the two halves of Guglielmo da Pisa's 12th-century pulpit, with carved reliefs depicting the life of Jesus. Transferred from Pisa Cathedral, the Cagliari work was split in two by the Catalans. Its stone lions are now on the choir stairs.

The cathedral's other art treasures include the *Clement VII Triptych* attributed variously to the school of Rogier van der Weyden or to Gerard David, and supposedly left by a remorseful Spanish soldier who had stolen it during the Sack of Rome in 1527.

Museums

On the Piazza Arsenale, the discreet modern architecture of the island's finest museum complex—*Cittadella dei Musei*—fits harmoniously into the Castello's medieval and Baroque setting. The Archaeological Museum houses Sardinia's ancient art and artefacts from prehistoric times to the Middle Ages. Exhibits offer a comprehensive introduction to the mysterious civilization of the *nuraghi*. Most remarkable are beautifully fashioned bronze figures found in the prehistoric villages' sacred wells, and the Phoenician and Roman sculpture, jewellery, ceramics and glassware.

In the Art Gallery—*Pinacoteca Nazionale*—the main interest is the series of altar paintings salvaged during the anti-clerical movement of the late 19th century. Most were executed by Catalan and afterwards by Sardinian artists in the 15th and 16th centuries, maintaining the sober International Gothic style long after Renaissance and Mannerist painters were dominating the Italian mainland. Among the Sardinian painters represented here are the pioneering Lorenzo Cavaro and Antioco Mainas.

The Cardu Museum is devoted to Thai, Chinese and Southeast Asian art, donated to Cagliari by a private collector.

About Town

Before and after the Pisans and Catalans, the city was active beyond its fortifications, as its

ABOUT TOWN

Along the palm-lined boulevards of modern Cagliari, the archaeological accent is on elegance.

monuments show. There are also some pleasant gardens in which to escape the city bustle.

San Saturno
Also known as Santissimi Cosma e Damiano, this fine 11th–12th century Provençal Romanesque edifice is, at its core, one of the oldest churches in Sardinia. At the southern end of Via Dante, it betrays its 6th-century Byzantine origins in the domed Greek-cross plan at the centre, the site where Saturnus was martyred during the reign of Emperor Diocletian. Early Christian remains are being revealed by ongoing excavations in the courtyard.

San Domenico
In keeping with the tradition of the Dominican order, their pilgrimage church was originally founded outside the city-centre (near Piazza Garibaldi). The Catalan Gothic edifice of the 15th century has been reconstructed since the bombardment of World War II, with remains of the old church now serving as the crypt. In the Rosario Chapel on the left-hand side is the standard hoisted by victorious Sardinian arquebusiers at the Battle of Lepanto against the Turks in 1571. Untouched by the bombs, the charming cloister is Renaissance on one side, Gothic on the other.

ABOUT TOWN

Gallery of Modern Art
The *Galleria Comunale d'Arte Moderna* is housed in a neoclassical villa at the north end of the Public Gardens. The gunpowder originally stored here has been replaced by Italian avant-garde sculpture and paintings of the 1960s and '70s and temporary exhibitions by Sardinian artists.

Roman Remains
From the Viale Fra Ignazio, on the north side of the excavations, you get a good view of the amphitheatre built in the 2nd century AD. Some 15,000 spectators could gather in the hillside's natural hollow to watch gladiators combat wild beasts shipped in from North Africa. Today, it provides a handsome setting for summer opera and drama.

South of the theatre, three Roman villas of the same period have been excavated on the other side of the Botanical Gardens. Known collectively as Casa Tigellio, they have some elegant mosaics in the *tablinum*, one of the rooms looking out on the atrium.

Botanical Garden
Stretching south of the amphitheatre in an area exploited by Phoenicians and Romans for mining, the *Orto Botanico* brings together tropical, sub-tropical and Mediterranean plants and trees. The rarer specimens are kept in a section accessible by arrangement with the custodians.

Phoenician Necropolis
Settlers from Carthage carved their tombs out of the rock on a hillside on the west side of town (entrance Via Vittorio Veneto). Begun in the 6th century BC, the *Necropoli di Tuvixeddu* was in turn used by the Romans until the 1st century AD. Some of the Phoenician tombs are decorated with portraits of the deceased or their deities.

---

3 THE THREE BEST PARADES In an effort to preserve tradition, people turn out on foot, horseback and in ox-carts in three outstanding costumed processions. The **Sagra di Sant'Efisio**, May 1, carries the effigy of martyred St Efisio from Cagliari to Pula. On the penultimate Sunday in May, the **Cavalcata Sarda** parades through the streets of Sassari. For the **Festa del Redentore** (Redeemer) at the end of August, the people of Nuoro make their way to the top of Monte Ortobene.

THE SOUTH
Iglesiente, Sarrabus

With the island's hotel and restaurant facilities concentrated mainly at the other end of the island, the south has been unjustly neglected. The Iglesiente and Sarrabus regions on either side of Cagliari have interesting archaeological sites, and beach resorts are developing fast along the coast.

Iglesiente

Since Phoenician and Roman times, the region southwest of Cagliari has been exploited for its silver, lead and other minerals—in the 20th century for coal, under Mussolini. But whereas the interior is now dotted with ghost towns and disused mineshafts, the coastal region offers a growing number of attractive resorts with fine sandy beaches and pleasant forests to explore in the hinterland, plus two picturesque off-shore islands, Sant'Antioco and San Pietro.

Nora

The ancient port city, founded by the Phoenicians around the 8th century BC and taken over by the Romans, was the island's first capital. Destroyed by Vandal and Arab invaders, it was subsequently abandoned.

Set on a coastal promontory 44 km (27 miles) from Cagliari, just off highway 195 south of the modern town of Pula, the archaeological site was excavated in 1952. Start out from the ruins of the Phoenician Temple of Tanit for a good overall view of the city. The best-preserved remains are from the Roman era: the theatre from the 1st century AD, a temple's six columns and altar near the paved area of the forum, porticoes of the public baths and, in a patrician house, a black, white and ochre mosaic depicting a nymph riding a dolphin.

Santa Margherita di Pula

Surrounded by groves of swaying pines, the beaches of this burgeoning resort of villas and luxury hotels offer first-class water sports facilities, windsurfing and swimming in unpolluted waters (a blessing after the forbidding industrial region closer to Cagliari). There is a good 18-hole golf course, and excursions are organized for horseback riding on the forested slopes of Monte Orbai.

Costa del Sud

The coast takes on a wilder, more romantic aspect further south,

The theatre is one of the best-preserved remains of the Roman city of Nora, part of which is now under water.

where the landscape changes suddenly from gentle greenery and sand dunes to secluded coves and craggy promontories.

Chia is a charming town set back from the shore, its villas half hidden in inviting clumps of fig trees. Looking out to sea, the Torre di Chia is one of many sturdy towers built by the Spanish in the 16th and 17th centuries as an early-warning system against Turkish pirates and other invaders. Nearby are vestiges of the ancient Phoenician town of Bithia.

Most spectacular of the promontories are Capo Spartivento and Capo Malfatano.

Sant'Antioco and San Pietro

Remains of an ancient bridge suggest that the causeway over to Sant'Antioco has been there at least since Roman times. The present town of Sant'Antioco is built on the ancient site of Sulcis, the thriving port founded by the Phoenicians in 750 BC for shipping the locally mined silver and lead. Vestiges of their acropolis and cemetery can be seen on the hill on which the parish church and an 18th-century Piedmontese castle now stand. The Archaeological Museum nearby includes some fine jewellery and sculpture. Also displayed are funerary urns, both originals and copies, at the *tophet*, a children's burial ground. It was long thought that the Phoenicians performed a ritual sacrifice of their first-born, but the modern view is that the tophet was a burial place of still-born babies or infants who died from natural causes.

The port of Calasetta has a pleasant sandy beach at the north end of the island. The ferry from here to San Pietro takes 30 minutes. The smaller island is wilder and much favoured by birdwatchers. Carloforte is a pretty fishing port with spotless white and pastel-coloured houses. In the seductive little coves, the beaches slope away steeply and are better for adult scuba diving than family bathing.

Sarrabus

The coastline east of Cagliari alternates long stretches of sandy beaches with sheer cliffs plunging abruptly into the sea. Inland, tucked among the Sarrabus mountains, are some interesting examples of prehistoric rock-cut tombs and *nuraghi*. On the seaward side of the coast road from Cagliari, four towers built by the Pisans and Catalans—Mortório, Cala Regina, Stelle and Su Fenugu—stand as reminders of the defences against pirate raids launched nonstop from North Africa from ancient times until the end of the 18th century.

Villasimius

This old fishing village is a burgeoning resort within easy reach of a wide variety of popular sandy beaches and more tranquil rocky coves. Prize possession of the town's cultural centre is a marble sculpture dating back to the 1st century AD. Until recently, this female figure found among the remains of an ancient Roman public bath was worshipped as a statue of the Virgin Mary.

One of the most attractive excursions is the 6-km (3.5-mile) drive out to Capo Carbonara, the southeastern tip of the island. The little harbour's star-shaped fortress was built in the 16th century. For bathing, choose between the fine white sands of Simius Beach east of the cape and the granulated sands of Spiaggia del Riso (Rice Beach) to the west. Nearby, you have the added attraction of prehistoric *domus de janas* tombs cut out of the rocks, a group of *nuraghi* and a dilapidated "giants' tomb". And take a cruise in a glass-bottomed boat for a look at the Mediterranean marine life on your way out to the little isles of Cavoli and Serpentara.

Costa Rei to Torre Salinas

To escape the summer crowds, there are several quieter coves and sandy beaches along this coast stretching north of Villasimius past Capo Ferrato. At Piscina Rei is a group of 20 megaliths, six of them standing upright, perhaps with a religious significance comparable to the menhirs and dolmen of Brittany and Stonehenge. The beaches on either side of the old watchtower, Torre Salinas, boast some of Italy's whitest sands and cleanest waters. At the marshy Colostrai lagoon, bird-watchers may spot heron, cormorant, purple moorhen and peregrine falcon.

Around Muravera

Trade along the Flumendosa river dates back to exchanges with the ancient Etruscans. Today, the valley's towns of Muravera, Villaputzu and San Vito are renowned for their traditional craftwork and local farm produce. This is the centre of the Sarrabus region's citrus fruits, among the best in Sardinia. Besides the hand-woven and embroidered table linen and carpets, you will find the famous *launeddas* flute. Only here and in the Oristano region is this ancient three-piped musical instrument, a survival of Roman times, still crafted. It plays a prominent part in the local religious festivals: for San Vito's patron saint in June, Muravera's Sant'Agostino in late August and Villaputzu's Santa Vittoria in mid-October.

Sarrabus Mountains

Between San Priamo and Cagliari, highway 125 winds past spectacular wild panoramas along the densely wooded river valley. Just outside San Priamo, north of the road looms the Asoru *nuraghe*, 7 m (22 ft) high. Above the Cannas river, the Arco dell'Angelo (Angel's Arch) is a colossal rock of rose-coloured granite. South of the highway is one of the principal mountains of the rugged Sarrabus, the Sette Fratelli (Seven Brothers), surprisingly only 1,023 m (3,355 ft) high. This is hunting ground for boar, hare, partridge and wild duck—but *not* the endangered species of local deer. North of the highway is the village of Burcei, where tradition-conscious mountain folk eke out a living from their cherry orchards.

Dolianova

Just 20 km (12.5 miles) north of Cagliari, this farming town is well known for its table olives, olive oil, *pecorino* cheese and sweet muscatel wines. But it is also worth a visit for the church of San Pantaleo, an intriguing blend of Romanesque, Pisan Gothic and even Islamic styles, notably in its arches and windows. Besides the handsome stone pulpit, a Roman sarcophagus and early Christian baptismal font attest to its ancient history.

THE WEST

Oristano, Tharros, Arborea, Barumini, Nuraghe Losa, Bosa

At the northern end of the fertile farmland of the Campidano plain, Oristano is set among lagoons. The rich variety of migrant birds make them popular with nature lovers. The ancient Phoenician-Roman site of Tharros is barely more than a stroll from the beach at Torre Grande, while the *nuraghe* at Barumini is an easy day-trip from the coast. Bosa's river port and hilltop castle make it one of Sardinia's most colourful towns.

Oristano

The town derives its name from Aristius, a Roman tax-collector responsible for this west-coast region, which in ancient times earned its income from the lagoon fisheries. But it remained very much a backwater compared with the nearby thriving trade centre of Tharros, until incessant pirate raids and malaria forced the citizens of Tharros to move to Oristano in 1070.

In the struggle between Pisans and Catalans for control of the province of Arborea, Oristano sided with the Catalans but also claimed an administrative autonomy under its heroine Eleonora. This led to centuries of economic neglect, and it is only now that the town has revived its fortunes, doubling its population in the second half of the 20th century (now 35,000).

Piazza Roma

The elongated irregular square is now the bustling city centre, but its massive rectangular Torre di San Cristoforo (1290) looms above the Porta Manna that was once the gateway to the old town.

Antiquarium Arborense

Southeast of Piazza Roma on Via Parpaglia, the municipal museum is housed in the 18th-century Palazzo Parpaglia. It displays prehistoric obsidian and metal implements and utensils, bronze statuary found at nearby *nuraghi* settlements, Phoenician tomb treasures and Roman ceramics and glassware excavated at Tharros.

Duomo

The Gothic cathedral, built in the 13th century, was reconstructed in Baroque style in 1721. Its octagonal campanile dates from the 15th century. In the interior, the only remaining Gothic vestige is the groin-vaulted Rimedio

Chapel in the right transept. To the right of the nave are a 14th-century polychrome wooden *Annunciation* by Nino Pisano and parts of a sculpted medieval marble pulpit showing *Daniel in The Lions' Den* and other Biblical scenes.

San Francesco
The neoclassical church was built in the 19th century to replace a Gothic church whose façade survives in part on the adjacent military recruiting office. Over the left altar is a masterly wooden Crucifixion by 15th-century Catalan-Sardinian sculptor Nicodemo.

Piazza d'Arborea
Facing the Palazzo Comunale, a marble statue (1881) honours the town's heroine, Eleonora d'Arborea, known as the *giudica* (governing magistrate), who in the 14th century defended her people against the feudal excesses of their Catalan rulers. (Her house is on Via Parpaglia, near the municipal museum.)

Nostre Sorelle del Carmine
This absolutely enchanting little church on Via del Carmine is a veritable jewel of Rococo architecture (1785). Its golden sandstone façade is graced by Ionic pilasters and a beautifully curving window beneath the coat of arms of the church's benefactor, the Marquis of Arcais. The oval interior is a luminous play of delicately coloured stucco and marble.

The Lagoons
Birds flock to the lagoons *(Stagni)* of Oristano from all over Europe and Africa. To the south of town, the Stagno di Santa Giusta and Stagno Pauli Maiori are havens for bittern, purple heron, coot and buzzard, fishing and nesting among the reeds and feathery tamarisk. Thousands of pink flamingo gather in the autumn on the Stagno di Mistras west of Oristano. At the Stagno di Cabras to the north, the ruddy shelduck can be heard honking—while local fishermen are silently netting the eel and mullet.

Santa Giusta
The town grew out of the Phoenician and later Roman city of Othoca which, like Oristano of which it is now a suburb, had prospered from fish and the farm produce of the Campidano plain. Traces of the ancient acropolis have been found on the mound on which the cathedral is built. This 12th-century Pisan-style Romanesque edifice is one of the most

The charming town of Bosa, calmly reflecting on its past.

handsome churches in Sardinia. The dignified construction enhances its golden sandstone façade with white marble and dark basalt. In the sober interior, the capitals and plinths of the columns have been taken from Roman monuments.

Marina di Torre Grande
A fine sandy beach, holiday villas and well-equipped hotels are making this an increasingly fashionable resort, just 15 minutes from Oristano. On the waterfront, the Torre Grande was erected by the Spanish in the 15th century.

Tharros
Serious excavations began in 1956 to uncover this most prosperous of west coast Phoenician port cities, founded around 730 BC. Its geographical position at the end of the Sinis peninsula gave it two ports, east and west, allowing boats to choose the more favourable according to the winds. Tharros merchants began trading with what is now Marseille, the Balearic islands and the Catalan coast. By 500 BC, reinforced by wealth from Carthage, their boats ranged across the Mediterranean to Cyprus and Egypt in the east and around the Atlantic coast as far as Cornwall and Ireland. The Roman conquest of 238 BC signalled the end of Tharros's golden era by diverting all its trading resources to Rome. Jewish merchants continued to make a living until the town was taken over by Christians in the 4th century AD. Repeatedly plundered by pirate raids over the centuries, the diocese moved first to San Giovanni in Sinis and then to Oristano.

In the main, the archaeological site reveals the later Roman city: a street of shops and taverns, a temple with two of its Corinthian columns restored, a monumental water cistern and public baths transformed by the early Christians into a basilica with a hexagonal stone baptismal font. Of the Phoenician city, you can see a temple with Doric half-columns hewn from the sandstone bedrock and, north of the main site, a children's burial ground, or *tophet*. The urns found here once contained the remains of stillborn infants consecrated to the Phoenician deities so that bereaved parents might have other children.

Arborea
Built from scratch in 1928, this town south of Oristano is something of a modern curiosity in a region devoted by the Italian Fascists to land reclamation and hydraulic engineering. Amid lagoons and canals, past avenues of eucalyptus, groves of pine and a

For centuries, Barumini's nuraghic fortress lay hidden beneath a crust of earth, preserving it from the elements.

monumental giant water-pump, the town's austere Rationalistic architecture is itself a monument to the regime's determination to impose its mark on the landscape. But it's no longer named Mussolinia.

Barumini

Southeast of Oristano (highway 131, exit Villasanta), Barumini's formidable *Su Nuraxi* complex was uncovered by land subsidence following massive floods in 1949. Begun perhaps as early as the 15th century BC, the central three-storey palace-like structure, with its well 20 m (65 ft) deep, was progressively reinforced over the centuries by a first ring of four towers, an outer rampart and beyond that a village of some 50 circular dwellings. Tombs found in the vicinity suggest that fortress was also occupied by the Romans.

Giara di Gesturi

More *nuraghi*, overgrown with dense shrubbery and cork oak, are scattered across this beautiful wild plateau northwest of Barumini. Amid the greenery, you may be lucky enough to witness a captivating spectacle when herds of semi-wild ponies, *Cavallini della Giara*, come to graze or drink in two big rainwater ponds retained in hollows of the basalt rock, Pauli Aba Mingiau and Pauli Oromeo.

Nuraghe Losa

Just off highway 131, about 30 km (20 miles) northeast of Oristano, this great black-basalt tower, more than 3,500 years old, is one of the island's major prehistoric monuments. It was subsequently surrounded by a triangular bastion with a tower at each corner, linked by a system of passageways. Though it may have originally been a mausoleum—*Losa* means "tomb" in Sardinian dialect—the Phoenicians, Romans and perhaps Byzantines, too, took it over as a fortress.

Bosa

North of Oristano, the road to Bosa is flanked by undulating dunes to the west and evocative silhouettes of *nuraghi* to the east. Torre Su Puttu and Torre du Pittinuri, their Catalan counterparts on the seaward side, can be climbed for splendid views of the coast. The resorts of S'Archittu and Santa Caterina di Pittinuri each nestle at the heart of their own bay.

River port and citadel, Bosa is one of the island's most charming towns. With ancient origins probably dating back to the 9th century BC, it prospered from its key position at the mouth of the Temo river, Sardinia's only navigable waterway. Even after the estuary silted up in the Middle Ages, separating the town from the sea, it remained a vital strategic "gateway" to the island. The feudal lords of the Malaspina dello Spino Secco family built a mighty fortress up on the Serravalle hill. The town was split into two: hugging the hillside in the upper town, *Sa Costa*, were the squat houses of those serving the castle lords; whereas in *Sa Piatta*, the lower town down by the river, the more independent-minded merchants, sailors and fishermen built taller dwellings. This division still gives Bosa its distinctive character.

Castello di Serravalle

Begun in 1112, the massive fortress of the Malaspinas is dominated on its northern corner by a great rose-hued stone tower of rough volcanic trachyte. Other square towers were added, as well as an outer wall of bastions, to turn the castle into a citadel covering the whole hilltop.

Nostra Signora di Regnos Altos

Sa Costa vassals were summoned to worship in this 13th-century church inside the castle grounds, being permitted no church of their own. A remarkable series of frescoes (around 1370) has recently been uncovered on three walls of the original chapel (the choir and apse are later additions). Some portray events in the lives of saints Martin, George, Constantine (and his mother Helen), Christopher and Louis of Toulouse; others depict the Annunciation, the Adoration of the Magi and the Last Supper.

Sa Piatta

Bosa's lower town is distinguished by its elegant 18th- and 19th-century patrician mansions with wrought-iron balconies, most notably along Corso Vittorio Emanuele running parallel to the river. Most imposing is the Palazzo Don Carlos on Piazza Costituzione. Even the façade of the Cattedrale dell'Immacolata seems to have been conceived more for a Rococo palace than for a church. The old town's main streets and side streets alike are attractively paved with cobblestones and slabs of basalt. The artisans here produce good-quality coral jewellery, lace and embroidery. The local olive oil and Malvasia wine also have a good reputation.

Sas Conzas

The leather tanneries and warehouses on the left bank of the Temo river have rightly been declared a national monument of industrial archaeology—best picture from the bridge.

San Pietro Extramuros

Also on the left bank, east of town, is Bosa's former cathedral, a venerable Romanesque edifice begun in 1062, with a 12th-century apse and campanile, and 13th-century façade. As shown by its pagan inscriptions, masonry for the apse was taken from an ancient Roman necropolis.

Bosa Marina

This modern resort out on the coast used to be Bosa's little fishing port. The beach is delightful. Recently linked to the marina by a causeway, Isola Rossa boasts a lighthouse and watchtower.

---

4 THE FOUR BEST CASTLES The island's invaders all erected fortresses to hold on to what they had conquered. In **Bosa**, the Malaspinas put up theirs in the 12th century; in **Castelsardo**, it started with the Genoese; the Citadel in **Cagliari** is mostly Catalan; the Pisans built the towering fortress in **Posada** and got it straight.

NORTHWEST
Alghero, Sassari, Romanesque Churches, Torralba, Porto Torres, Castelsardo, Perfugas

The rolling countryside of the La Nurra and Logudoro regions covering the northwest corner of the island is clearly marked by each of its masters. Torralba is the starting point of the prehistoric Valley of Nuraghi. The Roman port of Turris Libisonis is now Porto Torres. The splendid Romanesque churches are the work of the Pisans, just as their Genoese rivals made prosperous towns out of Sassari and Castelsardo. And Alghero has retained the Catalan character of its rulers, who bolstered the region's security with a formidable series of watchtowers along the coast.

Alghero
All is peaceful now, but if you approach the town from the sea, the promontory of its old town *(centro storico)* still looks as though it's girded for war with its perennial enemies. On the skyline, the Gothic towers and Baroque domes of the churches are tucked safely behind ramparts bristling with bastions to ward off any plundering pirate. These fortifications—and the churches behind them—are the solid precautions of the town's Catalan conquerors, supplanting the more modest construction of the Genoese. The latter were defeated and driven from the city in 1354, to be replaced by Catalan immigrants from Barcelona and the Balearic islands. Ever since, even though the Italians reasserted their rights to the island in 1720, Alghero has never relinquished its Catalan language and customs, creating an atmosphere of dignity and elegance that sets it apart from the rest of the island.

It also creates a slight problem with place-names, which are written in both Italian and Catalan. Palace is *Palazzo* or *Palau*, streets *Via* or *Carrer*, for instance.

The Ramparts
Before plunging into the historic heart of the town, take a stroll along its perimeter of 15th- and 16th-century bastions named after three explorers, Columbus, Marco Polo and Magellan.

Start at the southern end, at Torre de l'Espero Reial, the round Tower of the Royal Spur, also known as Torre Sulis after a local Sardinian patriot, Vincenzo Sulis. The tree-lined square here has lively café terraces and a couple of good restaurants. Walk west to the low, octagonal tower popularly known as Torre deis Cutxos, Dog Tower: it was once used as a municipal dog-kennel. At the promontory's northwest corner, the 18th-century Torre de la Polvorera used to be the town's gunpowder house, with behind it the dilapidated army barracks.

Porto Darsena
The fishing harbour is at the east end of Magellan Bastion. Walk round to the end of the jetty for a wonderful panorama of the ramparts and old city viewed from the sea. Then enter the old town through the sailors' gateway, the Porta a Mare.

Piazza Civica
A gallery from Porta a Mare leads directly into the main medieval town square, handsomely paved with granite slabs and cobblestones and surrounded by elegant shops and what were once the customs houses and Palazzo Comunale. Next to a charming old-fashioned café (excellent cakes), the august Gothic Palau d'Albis hosted the Spanish Habsburg Emperor Charles V on his visit to Alghero in 1541 en route for Africa. He took time off from smiling and waving to the crowds to inspect the fortifications and complain about their inadequacies.

Cattedrale
The Catalan Gothic style of the town's imposing cathedral is concealed behind its four-columned 19th-century neoclassical façade and Baroque transformations effected in the interior under Piedmontese rule. A portal and the octogonal dome and bell towers are of Catalan design.

Catalan Palaces
Alghero's Catalan Gothic character can best be seen in the patrician residences south of the cathedral. Along with some of the town's most fashionable boutiques on Via Carlo Alberto (or Carrer Maior, as you like), are the nicely restored Palau Llorino and Palau Ross, opposite the church of San Francesco. On Via Principe Umberto, take a look at the Palau Machin, and on Via Roma the Palau Guio i Doran.

San Michele
This late-17th-century building at the end of Via Carlo Alberto, is perhaps the most opulent of the Jesuits' Baroque churches in Sardinia. The brilliance of its coloured majolica dome is repeated in the sumptuous stucco interior. As you enter, look back at the beautiful wooden choir gallery over the doorway. There are also fine altar paintings, such as *Christ's Baptism*, and an exquisitely sculpted Crucifixion.

Jewish Quarter

Leading north from the cathedral, Via Sant'Erasmo was the centre of Jewish life until the expulsion of Jews and Muslims from Spanish territories in 1492. Prosperous merchants of the Carcassona family built their princely residence here, subsequently renamed Palau Reial and now undergoing restoration. One of the sidestreets bears the name Carrer dels Hebreus. The synagogue, on Piazza Santa Croce, was transformed by the Jesuits into Santa Croce church and then destroyed.

Torre del Portal

At the end of Via Roma, this massive gate-tower, also known as Porta a Terra, is frequently identified as Torre dels Hebreus, showing that it was paid for by subscription from the Jewish community. It was at this gate, the only one facing the island interior, that the town controlled, very strictly, passage of non-residents coming in from the countryside. Today, it houses a monument to Italy's war dead.

Grotta di Nettuno

Boats from Alghero's Porto Darsena harbour make a two-hour cruise around Capo Caccia to view this fascinating sea cave along with two others, Grotta Verde and Grotta dei Ricami. The route by road, 27 km (16 miles), also offers spectacular sea views. For a guided tour of the illuminated cave entrance and a close up of the stalagmites and stalactites, you must take the 650-odd steps cut in the rock of *L'Escala del Cabiriol* (Goat's Stairway). Traces of Stone Age cave dwellers (5000 BC) were found in the Grotta Verde. You can combine this trip with a refreshing dip in the sea in lovely Porto Conte bay.

Nuraghe di Palmavera

A 15-minute drive west of Alghero, this recently discovered prehistoric village groups some 50 houses around the central palace-tower. The latter was built around 1000 BC, and other towers and dwellings were added over the next 300 years. If you also want to spend some time at the beach, the most convenient is Spiaggia di Bombarde.

Anghelu Ruju

This necropolis of 36 prehistoric rock-cut tombs is just off the Porto Torres road, 9 km (6 miles) north of Alghero. It constitutes one of island's most important *domus de janas* (witches' house) burial grounds. Bronze Age artefacts excavated here in 1905 are on display in Cagliari's Archaeological Museum, but wall inscriptions can still be seen at the tomb entrances. The "houses" reproduce in miniature the form of prehistoric dwellings.

Sassari

The people of Sardinia's second city (population 125,000) have an urbane and cheerful sophistication not generally to be found elsewhere in Sardinia. They seem to dress a little more stylishly, spend longer on their café terraces, have a reputable university and are rapidly moving their economy from agricultural produce and manufacturing industries to the "cleaner" service sector. They express that incorrigible Italian phenomenon of inter-city rivalry in their wonder that Cagliari and not Sassari is the island's capital.

The town draws great civic pride from its centuries-old tradition as a commercial centre, ever since it displaced the nearby port city of what is now Porto Torres, beset in the Middle Ages by pirates and malaria. But entrepreneurial energies in the 19th century and again after World War II threatened to destroy the town's whole medieval fabric. The area around the cathedral and the busy main street, Corso Vittorio Emanuele II, was nicknamed "Piazza Demolizione" (now Piazza Mazzotti and still just a parking lot). Reason only recently prevailed to preserve some good representative buildings and monuments of the *centro storico*.

Around the Corso

Corso Vittorio Emanuele II divided the medieval city in two halves and is still the busiest shopping street in town. Traditionalists use its ancient dialect name of *Platha de Codinas* (Street of Stones), referring to its handsome paving—laid at a time when other city streets were covered in little more than mud. Set back from the street, halfway down, the neoclassical horseshoe-shaped Teatro Civico replaced the old town hall in the early 19th century. Some fine 15th-century Catalan Gothic houses, with blind ground-floor arcades and twin-mullioned windows, are to be seen on the corner of Via dei Corsi and signposted down Via Canopolo, at numbers 20 and 23.

Down by the railway station, the Corso widens out into Piazza Sant' Antonio, with a piece of the medieval fortifications including a crenellated tower. Inside the Baroque church of Sant'Antonio (1709) is a fine gilded and inlaid wooden altar-piece by Genoese artist Bartolomeo Augusto.

Fonte Rosello

This monumental Renaissance fountain stands at the bottom of a

Sassari

Castelsardo's citadel now harbours a museum devoted to the peaceful craft of straw-weaving.

stairway just north of Corso Trinità. Somewhat dwarfed now by Mussolini's gigantic viaduct nearby, the green-and-white marble rectangle has allegorical statues of the four seasons at each corner and lion's heads spouting water. It is crowned by an equestrian statue of Saint Gavin atop two intersecting arches.

Duomo di San Nicola

The cathedral is a disconcerting combination of bold Catalan Gothic flying buttresses and equally forthright Baroque side porches and façade. This was completed in 1723, the work of Lombard architects and sculptors. The interior remains Gothic, though its principal art works are 17th-century paintings of saints Cosma and Damian by Carlo Maratta and *The Last Supper* by Giovanni Marghinotti.

Piazza d'Italia

The grandiose neoclassical Palazzo della Provincia, seat of Sassari's provincial government (1880), presides over the modern hub of city life along with a pompous monument of King Vittorio Emanuele II. The vast square, a pasture for sheep before Sassari began to expand in the 19th century, is surrounded by banks, offices, restaurants and cafés—a perfect place for people-watching during the ritual *passeggiata* evening stroll.

Archeological Museum
Endowed in part by a Sardinian mining magnate, Giovanni Antonio Sanna, the Museo Nazionale Archeologico Sanna is remarkable chiefly for its wide-ranging collection of prehistoric art, bronze statuary and ceramics from the region's *nuraghi* and burial grounds, and Roman jewellery, glassware and ceramics. The painting gallery *(pinacoteca)* includes works by the Florentines, Matteo Rosselli and Piero di Cosimo, and a *Madonna and Child* by Venetian Bartolomeo Vivarini.

Romanesque Churches
Pisa's domination of northwestern Sardinia left its stamp on the countryside with a series of harmoniously designed Romanesque churches. From the end of the 11th century, Tuscan masons and sculptors were brought in to work with local craftsmen in the distinctive Pisan three-tiered style. Here are three of the best examples amid the green Logudoro hills.

Santissima Trinità di Saccargia
Just 7 km (4 miles) southeast of Sassari right on highway 597, the 12th-century church combines light limestone and dark volcanic basalt, with ceramic detailing on the lozenge and rose windows of the upper façade. It achieves a fine harmony between the projecting portico, the main basilica and the lofty rectangular campanile, 40 m (130 ft), at the rear. Inside, in the apse beyond the simple wooden-beamed nave without aisles, are 13th-century frescoes depicting the life of Jesus surrounded by angels and his apostles. The basilica was originally an abbey church of the Camaldolite order, and remains of the monastery can be seen nearby.

Sant'Antioco di Bisarcio
Perched majestically on a rocky spur some 16 km (10 miles) further east, this formidable fortress-church has a campanile built like a castle-keep. Begun in the 11th century, both Pisan and French in its architectural inspiration, it provided a reassuring redoubt for the local bishop.

San Pietro di Sorres
Consecrated in the 11th century, the church stands on a hill overlooking Torralba's Valley of Nuraghi southeast of Sassari. The contrast of white limestone and black trachyte arches and pilasters on the broad façade is repeated in the interior's columns, arches and rib vaulting.

Torralba

In the grounds, Benedictine monks have a workshop for restoring and binding old books and manuscripts.

Torralba

The town is the centre of the region's Valley of Nuraghi, one of the most important series of prehistoric structures on the island. Its museum makes an excellent introduction to a tour of the sites, with explanatory models of the nuraghic villages and displays of excavated artefacts and ceramics. In the courtyard is a fascinating exhibit devoted to the Romans' road-building, including their milestones with Latin inscriptions.

Santu Antine

The biggest of the valley's prehistoric complexes has a central dry-stone tower of massive hewn basalt blocks, 17 m (55 ft) high. It was originally much taller, but the masonry of the rooftop balustrade was carried off in the 19th century by the good people of Torralba to build the village well—with mortar. Dating from around 1300 BC, it is surrounded by three later, smaller towers linked by a series of corridors and trenches.

Inside the central tower, a spiral ramp leads up to the rooms on higher levels. These may have been burial chambers in prehistoric times, but their impeccable state of repair encouraged the Romans to turn the place into a fortress. Its imposing appearance prompted early Christians to regard it as a royal palace, *Sa Domo de Su Rei*, the ruler being the sainted Emperor Constantine, whence the *nuraghe*'s present name.

Porto Torres

The ancient Roman trading port, Turris Libisonis, is now an important industrial port city for the products of its oil refineries. The Romans made it the northern terminus of their north-south road, a route still linking Cagliari and Porto Torres, the "Carlo Felice".

Roman Remains

Besides traces of the Roman road's ancient paving, the town has unearthed remains of the public baths, with some interesting polychrome mosaics, near the railway station, and a Roman bridge on the Mannu river. The archaeological collections on display in the Antiquarium Turritano include mosaics and other treasures excavated with difficulty during the town's modern industrial expansion.

San Gavino

Built at the beginning of the 11th century, the limestone basilica is considered to be the oldest of

Sardinia's Romanesque edifices. It stands on a mound that was originally a Roman necropolis. Unique among the island's churches, and rarely seen elsewhere in Italy, it has two apses with entrances on the side walls instead of a façade.

The church commemorates the martyrdom of St Gavin and shelters in its crypt, along with three Roman sarcophagi, the remains of Christians martyred during the persecutions at Emperor Diocletian at the beginning of the 4th century AD.

Platamona
This resort is very popular with residents of Sassari and Porto Torres, but it may seem too crowded and polluted for people with access to beaches further along the coast.

Monte d'Accoddi
West of the Sassari highway, 6 km (3.5 miles) from Porto Torres, the pyramidal ziggurat erected more than 4,000 years ago is the oldest of all Sardinian monuments. Nothing like this sacrificial altar, reminiscent of sanctuaries in Mesopotamia (modern Iraq), has been found anywhere else in the western Mediterranean. The megalithic altar-table standing at the top of a ramp was the setting for agricultural fertility rituals.

Castelsardo
Originally Castel Genovese and then Castel Aragonese, the imposing citadel makes this port town a popular resort long after its strategic importance has disappeared. The castle houses a fascinating museum devoted to straw-weaving *(intreccio)*, demonstrating how this ancient art is used not only for baskets but also for watertight boats, huts and the toughest of ropes. In the narrow streets of the medieval centre, women sit outside their doorways weaving baskets for the tourist trade.

A favourite curiosity on the way out of town on highway 134 is the *Roccia dell'Elefante*, a large rock eroded in the shape of a baby elephant brandishing its trunk over the road.

Perfugas
Some 30 km (18 miles) southeast of Castelsardo, the town has a fascinating museum displaying flint tools and weapons found in the silt of the nearby Altana river—the earliest traces left by human beings in Sardinia, dating from 150,000 BC. Other exhibits include fossilized vegetation from the region's petrified forest, 15 *million* years old, and later prehistoric remains, notably a small fertility goddess modelled from loam and artefacts from the *nuraghe*.

NORTHEAST

Olbia, Posada, Costa Smeralda, North Coast Resorts, Maddalena Islands, Gallura

In recent years, the once wild and almost deserted northeast coast, home of a few fishermen with a couple of shepherds here and there in the hinterland, has become one of the most desirable resort areas in the Mediterranean. For the well-heeled sailing fraternity, water sports enthusiasts and other more indolent holidaymakers, Costa Smeralda around Porto Cervo has blossomed into an enchanted playground.

Encouraged by its success, other resorts, from Porto Rotondo on one side to Baia Sardinia and Santa Teresa Gallura on the other, have sprung up along the rugged coastline enhanced by a profusion of brilliant Mediterranean shrubs among some often astonishing rock formations. The translucent, unpolluted waters really are emerald green—but also in places sparkling turquoise or sapphire blue. The offshore islands have long served as refuges, Maddalena for pirates, Caprera for the national hero Giuseppe Garibaldi, but these, too, are now prospering as holiday resorts. The topography of the coast's wind-sculpted cliffs extends into the mountainous terrain of the Gallura interior.

Olbia

As the island's busiest passenger port—with a growing airport—Olbia provides easy access to the Costa Smeralda and other resorts on the northeast coast. Despite its Greek name, the town is of Phoenician origin and was subsequently developed for trade by the Romans. A viaduct of the coastal highway 125 spans the old Roman port north of the present-day ferry docks. Vestiges of the ancient necropolis can be seen near the church of San Simplicio. This 11th–12th century Pisan Romanesque edifice, austerely built in handsome Gallura granite, makes use of columns and other masonry from pagan Roman and Phoenician temples in its interior. In the side aisles are ancient funerary urns, milestones and tombstones with Latin inscriptions.

Posada

About 50 km (30 miles) south of Olbia, Posada occupies an enchanting position on a limestone promontory crowned by a medieval castle, with small white houses spilling down the hillside. The Castello della Fava is dominated by a square tower 20 m

(65 ft) high, with a splendid view over the Posada river estuary and the white peaks of Monte Albo to the southwest. A few minutes' drive further south lies the beach resort of La Caletta, popular for its fine white sands. Drive a little further still for the pretty fishing village of Santa Lucia.

Costa Smeralda

Some 30 km (18 miles) north of Olbia, this now world-famous stretch of Sardinia's coastline was "discovered" by Prince Karim Aga Khan IV, the fabulously wealthy entrepreneur and spiritual head of the Ismaili sect of Islam, while cruising the area in his yacht in the 1950s. He was struck by the region's unspoiled charms and found a group of businessmen to join him in developing it as a resort area that would protect its natural beauty.

Every precaution has been taken to merit its now consecrated label of "millionaire's playground". With Porto Cervo at its centre, the coastline stretches just 55 km (34 miles) along more than 80 bays, rocky coves and sandy beaches. The villas, hotels, sports clubs, harbour facilities and whole villages built since the 1960s in this hitherto practically uninhabited area have all been designed to respect the spirit of the land. Using local granite and limestone, architects usually give their modern variations of Tuscan, Venetian or "Sardinian-rustic" housing an apparent patina of age, often in subtle pastel tones of ochre or russet, to preserve the landscape from any jarring newness. No roof can rise higher than the surrounding trees. The Mediterranean vegetation is lovingly protected, the maquis of myrtle, heath, juniper, tamarisk, cork oak and ilex that frames the granite cliffs. Equal respect is afforded the fauna: captains of industry; media magnates; film and rock stars; crowned heads of small principalities. And the emerald quality of the water is maintained by sophisticated purification plants and severe restrictions on pollution.

Porto Cervo

The capital of Costa Smeralda commands its northern tip. It has all the requisites of any self-respecting millionaire's playground: marinas; yacht club; tennis club (with ATP-rated professional on hand to coach); golf course; gourmet supermarket, perfume and jewellery shops; high-fashion casual-wear boutiques; restaurants and cafés on the Piazzetta; and a newspaper shop to pick up the daily delivered *Wall Street Journal*, *Financial Times* and *International Herald Tribune*—for business remains business, even on holiday. The town has existed long enough for there to be a Porto Vecchio (Old Port) with a ferry service over to the Marina across Porto Cervo Bay, moorings for 650 yachts. The flotilla is at its most impressive in mid-August. There is also a church, the Stella Maris, to which local benefactors have donated a 16th-century Neapolitan organ, a German Baroque altar cross and a *Madonna Dolorosa* attributed to El Greco.

The Beaches
Many of the best beaches are accessible only by boat—among the more select, the remote coves of Capo Ferro, the pink sands of Spiaggia della Rosa or the Isle of Mortório. Along the east coast, Cala di Volpe (Fox Cove) and Capo Capriccioli offer both white sands and rocky coves with shade from venerable olive trees. Just north of Porto Cervo, the little resort of Liscia da Vacca has its own beach.

Porto Rotondo
Nestling in its own little bay at the edge of a peninsula south of Costa Smeralda, this very elegant resort is perhaps less "exclusive" but is still much appreciated for the cosy village atmosphere and smart shops. It has first-class water sports facilities and excellent beaches for family bathing.

North Coast Resorts
In the wake of Costa Smeralda's success, other resorts have mushroomed further up the coast. What they sometimes lack in prestige—and in expense—they make up for in easier access to the beautiful rugged landscape and a more relaxed family atmosphere.

Baia Sardinia
Its pretty sailing harbour, fine sandy beaches and grand view of the Maddalena islands have made this one of the most popular resorts in the region. At sunset, the stylish ambience on the Piazza matches anything to be seen at Costa Smeralda's Porto Cervo.

Palau
Embarkation-point for cruises to the Maddalena islands, this bustling little port also has a good beach of its own. Its main attraction is the nearby Capo d'Orso (Bear Cape) on a headland 5 km (3 miles) east of town. An exhilarating climb over a well-marked path among the rocks brings you to a formidable rock formation in the shape of a great grizzly bear poking its mighty head out over the cliffs.

Porto Pozzo
Characteristic for the region, the town combines farming activities in the hinterland, including

NORTHEAST

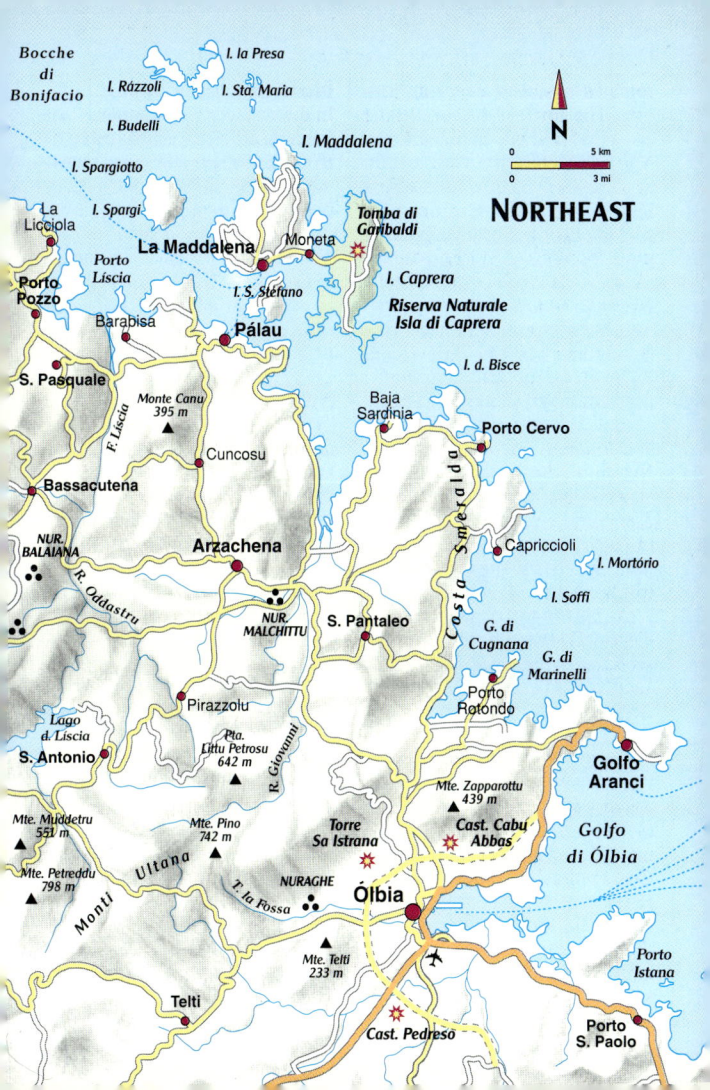

some reputable olive oil, with fishing from its harbour. Water sports enthusiasts appreciate the nearby beaches of Erica, La Licciola and La Marmorata, where the sea is a brilliant green-blue and its marine life a delight for scuba divers.

Santa Teresa Gallura
This burgeoning seaside resort—population 4,200 in winter, more than 40,000 in summer—benefits from a whole range of landscapes: the evergreen shrubbery and stunted trees of the Mediterranean maquis, sandy beaches and rocky coves overhung with dramatic expanses of fissured granite and giant boulders eroded into fantastic shapes, as at spectacular Punta Falcone east of town. Just 12 km (7 miles) across the Bocche di Bonifacio can be seen the white cliffs of Corsica.

Capo Testa
Out on the wild promontory 5 km (3 miles) west of Santa Teresa, shared by a deserted military radar station and a colony of black cats, the granite was quarried by Emperor Hadrian's Romans for his Pantheon and by Pisans for their cathedral. Down below, on Cala Spinosa, British sculptor Henry Moore carved the white stone for his semi-abstract figures, some of which he has left behind on the beach.

Costa Paradiso
Between the watchtower of Vignola and the fishing port of Isola Rossa, popular tourist villages and camping sites take advantage of the romantic ruggedness of the coastline, enhanced by coral-hued rock that blushes almost red at sunset. The mussels and other shellfish here are highly prized by the island's gourmet restaurants.

Maddalena Islands
The archipelago owes much of its romantic reputation to the rogues and heroes who have found a haven here—pirates, political refugees and freedom-fighter Giuseppe Garibaldi. A quieter crowd hangs out there now: sailing and other water sports enthusiasts at the tourist villages on La Maddalena, bird-watchers and Garibaldi pilgrims on Caprera. Just 15 minutes by ferry from Palau, these two are linked by a walkable causeway, while most of the other five islands are uninhabited. The United States Navy parks its nuclear submarines between Santo Stefano and La Maddalena. Film buffs should know that Michelangelo Antonioni shot his bizarre *L'Avventura* on the isle of Budelli.

La Maddalena
The largest of the seven islands covers 20 sq km (almost 8 sq

MADDALENA ISLANDS

Lovers of water sports are spoiled in every coastal resort, but the winds are best off the northern shores.

miles). The harbour and Piazza Garibaldi are at their liveliest during the evening *passeggiata*. In the parish church of Santa Maria Maddalena are two monumental candlesticks and a silver crucifix left here by Admiral Horatio Nelson before setting sail to his famous victory over the French at Trafalgar. La Maddalena was generally not a successful place for the French. At the nearby fishing harbour of Cala Gavetta, the Piazza XXIII Febbraio 1793 commemorates the islanders' successful resistance to French efforts to seize the archipelago—the assault force included Napoleon Bonaparte.

Caprera

The island's rough, tough terrain attracted rough, tough Giuseppe Garibaldi in 1854, after years in exile in South America and an abortive first attempt to unite Sardinia with Italy in 1848. His home and museum, *Compendio Garibaldino*, assembles memorabilia, sculptures, paintings and documents. His simple granite tomb is flanked by those of his sons and wife, Anita. The east side of the island around Cala Coticcio is accessible only by boat, but here bird-watchers can spot the peregrine falcon, tufted cormorant and the region's rarer gulls, royal and Corsican.

Gallura

The northeast interior has all the attributes of mountains—giddy crags, plunging ravines, deep valleys and steep slopes—everything except altitude, for the land rarely rises above 700 m (2,300 ft). The local granite, used in prehistoric times for *tombe dei giganti* (giants' tombs), has since made for some good-looking churches and palazzi.

Arzachena

With the emergence of the Costa Smeralda as a major tourist destination, this once sleepy village is now a busy service-oriented town handling the infrastructure of the region's tourist industry. It is surrounded by a host of fascinating prehistoric monuments.

A short drive south of town on the road towards Luogo Santo are two of the island's best-preserved *tombe dei giganti*—Coddhu' Ecchju and Li Lolghi—dating perhaps back to 3000 BC. Guarding the entrance to the tombs is a tall granite megalith. The tomb enclosure at Coddhu' Ecchju measures 15 m (49 ft) in length, big enough for 30 or 40 bodies. Also nearby is a good example of a *nuraghe*, La Prisgiona.

Tempio Pausania

This centuries-old administrative rival to Olbia is a centre of cork manufacturing and wine production—notably muscatel and Vermentino. Besides the surrounding vineyards and cork-oak forests, its climate and mineral waters make it an attractive starting point for bracing hikes into the Gallura mountains. The granite plateau on which the town is built has furnished the materials for the Cattedrale and the adjacent Oratorio del Rosario. With some reconstruction in the 19th century, they make a harmonious combination of late Romanesque and Baroque elements in the façades and interior.

---

5 THE FIVE BEST NURAGHI With 7,000 to choose from, here are the most impressive of these unique prehistoric structures: the three-storey tower at **Barumini**; the mausoleum-like **Nuraghe Losa** near Abbasanta; the Sant'Antine complex in the Valley of Nuraghi at **Torralba**; the picturesque prehistoric village of **Serra Orrios**; and the 50 dwellings of **Palmavera** near Alghero.

THE CENTRE
Nuoro, Oliena, Barbagia, The Coast

This is the unconquered heart of Sardinia. In Roman times, Emperor Tiberius sent in 4,000 hardened criminals and political prisoners to combat the assaults of herdsmen and bandits from the Gennargentu mountains, all to no avail. Justinian had to set up permanent garrisons in the foothills to stem the tide of a region he dubbed *Barbaria*. The term of contempt—*Barbagia* in Sardinian dialect—has today become the mountain folk's badge of honour. In times of hardship, some have resorted to banditry, stealing cattle from each other, raiding farm villages, kidnapping the landlords' children. Today, this image of mountain bandits is sustained only by extravagant tourist brochures to give visitors a cheap thrill. The shepherds and other mountain dwellers, few and far between, remain proudly aloof.

Nuoro, the provincial capital, maintains the region's traditions and culture at the northern edge of the Barbagia. Oliena, centre of a much esteemed wine region, has some of island's finest craftsmen, and ramblers enjoy the nearby Sopramonte hills. The east coast resorts offer spectacular scenery and quiet beaches.

Nuoro

Although it lacks an illustrious history, Nuoro is the staunchest custodian of Sardinia's old ways of life, remaining relatively free from Italian mainland or even more "cosmopolitan" influences. Many people here still wear their traditional costume at Sunday mass. Religious festivals like the Sagra del Redentore are observed with meticulous care. It is no accident that Nuoro was the home town of Grazia Deledda, the first Italian woman to win the Nobel Prize for Literature, with her uncompromising, by no means romantic accounts of Sardinian rural and small town life.

The first historical mention of Nuoro is in 1342, when it was the region's highest tax-payer. It slumbered as a feudal backwater until the 19th century, when uprisings against exploitation by landowners erupted in full-scale revolt in 1868. The church helped to build new schools—and a cathedral—and it became provincial capital in 1927.

City Centre
The attractive, granite-paved streets of Via La Marmora and Corso Garibaldi run through the heart of the city's shopping area.

The cafés and bars here and on the Piazza Vittorio Emanuele II are the lively focus of the evening *passeggiata*.

Folklore Museum

On Sant'Onofrio hill south of the cathedral, the *Museo della Vita e delle Tradizioni Popolari Sarde* is considered the island's best collection of costumes, jewellery, furniture and artefacts of Sardinian daily life at the end of the 19th century. Opened in 1976, it is housed in an attractively designed group of buildings around a courtyard, reminiscent of a traditional Sardinian village. Among the more intriguing exhibits are the eerie masks and costumes used in Barbagia carnival processions, and all the different forms of bread and various sweetmeats linked with annual festivities.

Continue on up through the trees on Sant'Onofrio hill for a fine view over the town and surrounding mountains.

Santa Maria della Neve

The neoclassical cathedral with a campanile on either side of its Ionic-columned façade was completed in 1854. Inside, among mostly 20th-century paintings, *Jesus' Dispute in the Temple* is a 17th-century work attributed to the Neapolitan studio of Luca Giordano.

Archaeological Museum

The *Civico Museo Speleo-Archeologico* displays the region's most important finds of fossils, bones and tools of early Stone Age cave dwellers, dated at 15,000 BC.

Museo Deleddiano

The home of Nuoro's very own Nobel Prize winner (1871–1936) has been turned into a museum, Via Grazia Deledda 28. Besides the writer's personal belongings, old photographs and first editions of her books, the rooms and courtyard tastefully recreate the rural atmosphere she describes in her autobiographical book, *Cosima*.

Monte Ortobene

The hilltop site of Nuoro's religious pilgrimages, 955 m (3,132 ft), is on the east side of town. From the Via Aspromonte, the winding Viale Ciusa climbs past the little church *(chiesetta)* della Solitudine, where Grazia Deledda is buried. The panoramic route continues 7 km (4 miles) up through granite boulders eroded into bizarre shapes, framed by a dense vegetation of heath shrubs, holm, cork and English oak trees.

Bare walls are a challenge to the mural painters of Barbagia. Here, a street corner in Aritzo.

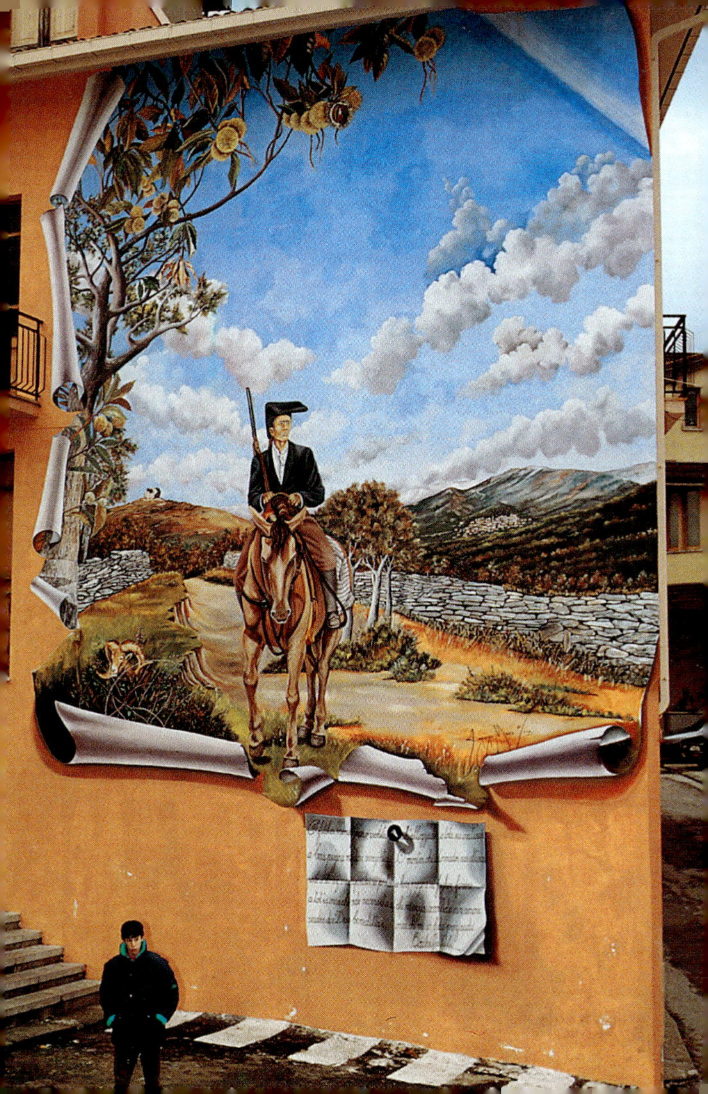

At the top, among more recently planted conifers, is the church of Nostra Signora di Montenero (1608) with the modern bronze statue of the Redeemer *(Redentore)*. At the end of August, this is the scene of one of Sardinia's most important traditional folk festivities. The music, dance and traditional costumes draw people from all over the island. The rest of the year, the excursion is worthwhile for the splendid view east to Monte Albo and, for a foretaste of any tour of the Barbagia, south over the peaks of the Gennargentu.

Oliena

Many of the old Sardinian customs for which its neighbour and rival Nuoro has set itself up as a guardian are put into practice here. Mainland Italians praise its heady, fruity Cannonau wines. Oliena artisans are renowned for their filigree silver and gold jewellery and delicately embroidered silk shawls. And architects from the Costa Smeralda come to copy the old houses for their ingenious designs, immaculately whitewashed, with exterior stairways, balconies, terraces and bizarre little chimney pots. Equally graceful are the churches, 11 in all for less than 8,000 inhabitants. Besides the charming old 13th-century Romanesque church of Santa Maria and the Jesuits' 18th-century Sant'Ignazio di Loyola, look out for the Santa Croce with its exquisite little campanile, on Via Deledda.

Sopramonte

If you don't mind the short but dizzyingly sinuous drive up the mountain immediately south of Oliena, there are some beautiful walks to be taken through the holm oaks of the Maccione forest. On the white limestone heights of Punta Corrasi, bird-watchers may be fortunate enough to spot rare specimens of bearded or griffon vultures.

Su Gologone Waterfalls

Just 5 km (3 miles) east of Oliena, a side-road leads to the cascade in a romantic forest. A boardwalk and rocky ledge take you right up to where the underground mountain stream pours out among the cliffs—with a reputed restaurant nearby.

Serra Orrios

Some 20 km (12 miles) east of Nuoro south of highway 129, this prehistoric village of *nuraghi* derives much of its charm from its setting amid wild olive trees and mastic bushes. You get a sense of a real village while walking among its clusters of round huts with courtyards and alleys leading to the communal water cisterns and wells. Two larger rectangular buildings may have been temples, built in part from massive basalt megaliths.

Barbagia

A complete tour of the central region of the Barbagia could take several days. For a first taste, we suggest here a day-trip immediately south of Nuoro to the central Gennargentu mountains.

Orgosolo

From Nuoro, the road follows the meanders of the Cedrino river about 20 km (12 miles) south to what is popularly recognized as the "capital" of the Barbagia. The region's most notorious bandits are said to have taken refuge along the town's steep and narrow little streets. Today, it is home to the proud and silent fraternity of shepherds. Scores of colourful modern murals on their rustic houses portray the struggle to preserve their local culture.

For religious festivals, the womenfolk bring out their best traditional costume, with brightly embroidered smocks and saffron silk scarves that reveal only their eyes. The most notable celebration is on Assumption Day, August 15, when the procession starts out from the 16th-century Assunta church. The men, also in costume, parade on horseback and perform acrobatic feats at the end of the procession.

Forest of Montes

For a ramble through some of Europe's most beautiful stands of giant holm oak, take the road that winds 18 km (11 miles) south to Funtana Bona, a granite plateau at 1,082 m (3,548 ft). You may spot some of the wild short-fleeced mouflon sheep, a protected species being nurtured by the forestry station. Over to the east, sheer cliffs of barren rock soar above the forest up to the peak of Monte Novo San Giovanni, 1,316 m (4,316 ft).

Mamoiada

Some of the more prosperous herdsmen's houses in this medieval village have retained their Catalan Gothic windows and doors. Inside the parish church of Our Lady of Loreto, beneath its impressive dome, are some delightful rustic frescoes. Decidedly less cheerful is the town's famous *Mamuthones* procession for the pre-Lent Carnival, when the men don heavy sheepskin cloaks and fearful wooden masks and parade slowly through the town tolling clusters of mournful bells. (Their procession is well exhibited in Nuoro's Folklore Museum.)

Fonni

The highest town on the island, 1,000 m (3,280 ft) above sea level, is built on a granite plateau

A timeless scene in the pastures near Oliena. The ewes' milk is used for pecorino and ricotta cheese.

at the northern edge of the Gennargentu mountains. It gets enough snow for some cross-country skiing and a little modest downhill in winter, and cooler summer temperatures to make it a refreshing resort in July and August.

Surrounding the late Gothic parish church of San Giovanni Battista, the city centre's older houses make attractive use of the local granite. But the town's most noteworthy landmark is the Madonna dei Martiri basilica with its adjoining Franciscan monastery. Originally built in the early 17th century, the church was remodelled in monumental Baroque style in 1716 to receive the extraordinary Madonna dei Martiri. This figure was fashioned in Rome from a compounded mixture of the crushed bones and other relics of various ancient martyrs. On the large square in front of the church are the rustic hostels built to receive the thousands of pilgrims drawn to worship the revered figure.

Two Mountains

Fonni is "base camp" for climbing the island's two highest peaks—Bruncu Spina, 1,829 m (6,000 ft), and Punta La Marmora, 1,834 m (6,015 ft). In fact, the lazy can drive most of the way up Bruncu Spina, to the S'Arena mountain refuge at 1,500 m (4,920 ft), and then take a relatively easy hike to the top. Punta La Marmora is more strenuous, but climbers say the reward, a view over the *whole* island, is well worth it.

The Coast
On the way to the central region's east coast, Dorgali is an important centre for traditional craftwork, especially carpet-weaving, leather goods and gold jewellery. Gourmets appreciate its *pecorino* cheese and the local Cannonau wines. It is also the northern starting point for two winding panoramic roads to the sea.

Cala Gonone
Originally a fishing port and embarkation for Dorgali's wines and cheeses, the town is now a growing resort. It offers cruises to secluded sandy beaches and rocky coves accessible only by boat. A major attraction to the south is the spectacular Grotto di Bue Marino, with its freshwater ponds and subterranean, cathedral-like vaults, a haven for Mediterranean monk seals in the late spring. Their name in local dialect, *boe marinu*, means literally, sea ox.

Arbatax
One of Sardinia's most picturesque mountain roads runs 64 km (40 miles) south from Dorgali to this popular beach resort, famous for its jagged red porphyry cliffs and rocky outcliffs making a brilliant contrast with the clear turquoise sea. You get a superb view of the coast from Capo Bellavista lighthouse. The modern hotels at this ferry port offer excellent facilities for water sports.

---

6 THE SIX BEST CHURCHES On the outskirts of Oristano **Santa Giusta** is a Romanesque jewel. Horizontal stripes of light limestone and dark basalt highlight **Santissima Trinità di Saccargia** near Sassari. In Bosa, the frescoes are the attraction at the castle's **Nostra Signora di Regnos Altos**. At Porto Torres, **San Gavino** is a rare example of a two-apse church. **San Saturno** in Cagliari dates back to earliest Christian times. The Benedictine monks are still working at **San Pietro di Sorres** near Torralba.

CULTURAL NOTES

Church Architecture
Sardinia's invaders imposed their own characteristic styles. Pisan Romanesque was inspired by Pisa's own cathedral, working variations on a façade of three tiers of open or blind arcades above three porches, and a campanile with arcaded windows. Catalan Gothic took its cue from Barcelona Cathedral, featuring interiors with very wide and high naves, and aisles often replaced by chapels between internal buttresses. The island's Baroque churches followed the Spanish Jesuits' taste for elegance and power. They were succeeded by the cooler neo-classical Grecian styles brought in by the Piedmontese in the 19th century.

Cork
The island's flourishing cork industry got its first real boost when French wine-bottlers came to prospect Sardinia's vast stands of cork oaks in the 1830s.

In its natural state, the *Quercus suber* grows only in the Western Mediterranean. These hardy trees favour the hard, dry soil of granite and volcanic trachyte plateaux, the best up on the northern Gallura and south of the Barbagia on the Giara di Gesturi. A cork oak can live up to 300 years and reach a height of 20 m (65 ft). The initially pale greyish-brown bark needs to be stripped with care, to avoid scarring the trunk's red-brown bole so that new bark can grow back again. Starting with a five-year-old tree, the cork-bark can be stripped up to eight times, at ten-year intervals, before the quality of cork deteriorates.

In the cork factories of Tempio Pausania and Callangianis, inferior cork is sorted out to be ground down as insulating material in buildings. The good stuff is left outdoors for six months for sun and rain to bleach out impurities. It is then boiled in vats to remove tannic acids and give it elasticity. Besides wine corks, the material serves as shoe soles, wall coverings, table mats, cocktail coasters and other staples of the souvenir industry.

Grazia Deledda
More than any other Sardinian in history, the winner of the Nobel Prize for Literature in 1926 made the rest of Italy, if not the whole world, aware of the distinctive nature of the island's way of life. Born in Nuoro in 1871 of a moderately well-to-do family, her exceptional intelligence and independent spirit quickly exhausted her school and private teachers. At 15, she published in a scholarly maga-

zine of Italian ethnography a detailed study of her region's customs. When she reworked the material in novel-form, she shocked the good people of Nuoro with her revelations of local superstitions, oaths and curses, painting a picture of Sardinia that was often more pagan than Christian. She married and moved to Rome in 1900, but never lost contact with her native island, which remained her basic source of inspiration, enhanced by sharp psychological insights. Among her best-known novels are *After the Divorce*, *Ashes* and *The Mother*. Grazia Deledda is buried at the Chiesetta della Solitudine on Monte Orbene, above Nuoro.

Giuseppe Garibaldi
In between fighting for freedom in various South American countries and on the Italian mainland, the great patriot (1807–82) liked fishing in Sardinia. He was born in Nice and as a youth went to sea in the Sardinian navy. From 1836 to 1846, he learned guerrilla warfare with rebels in Brazil and Uruguay and came back to use the tactics in Italy, at first unsuccessfully, against the armies of the Austrian Habsburgs and the French. In 1854, he built a home on the Isle of Caprera before resuming the struggle for Italian unity at the head of his 1,000 Red Shirts. Good soldier, bad politician, he retired disgruntled to his Caprera home and died there in 1882.

Murals
This late-blossoming folk art began in Sardinia in the 1970s. Paintings by individuals or groups cover vast wall-surfaces with social and political themes. Naïve in style but progressive in subject, they usually emphasize Sardinian local patriotism, unemployment, the encroachment of modern materialism, oppressive factory-owners and the rural exodus into the cities or overseas. Centres of the art include Orgosolo, Ozieri, Oliena, Alghero and Nuoro.

National Politicians
For some reason, Sardinia has produced more than its fair share of 20th-century politicians. Cofounder of the Italian Communist Party and its most enlightened theoretician, Antonio Gramsci (1891–1937) was born in Ales, western Sardinia. He died after 11 years of incarceration in Mussolini's jails, where his writings made him the champion of anti-Stalinist Marxists. Sassari produced two Italian Presidents—Antonio Segni and Francesco Cossiga—and another Communist Party leader, Enrico Berlinguer (1922–84), a liberal-minded patrician.

Shopping

The island has revived traditional carpet-weaving, jewellery, pottery and other cottage industries promoted by ISOLA, l'Istituto Sardo per l'Organizzazione del Lavoro Artigiano. Founded in 1957, it has shops in all the main towns.

Where?

Before shopping around in boutiques and souvenir shops, compare prices and quality of craftware in ISOLA outlets in Cagliari, Nuoro, Porto Cervo, Oristano, Alghero and especially Sassari which has a big shop in its Giardini Pubblici. The range of goods offered here is especially good, and you can be sure you are looking at the genuine article. Elsewhere, Castelsardo, Bosa and the island of Sant' Antioco are well known for their craftsmanship.

What?

Your best bets are the products that the Sardinians themselves esteem, after centuries of use.

The classical example is the shepherd's pocket-knife. This is an object of pride, hand-forged and honed, razor-sharp, pointed like a *foll'e murta* (myrtle leaf), with a handle of polished deer horn. The best are made at Pattada in the Logudoro region.

Local sources of coral have long been exhausted, but the traditional skills have not died out, also applied now to finely crafted gold and silver jewellery. Gold and silver filigree remains a Sardinian speciality.

Bosa is famous for its lace. For carpets, try Alghero, Santu Lussurgiu and northern towns in the Gallura. Oliena produces superb embroidered silk shawls.

On the Costa Smeralda, the modern resort of Porto Cervo has made its contribution with a ceramics workshop for traditional and new styles.

Basketware and other straw goods are especially prized at Castelsardo.

You might also like to consider taking home some gourmet products—Cannonau or sweet Malvasia dessert wines from Oliena or around Oristano, *pecorino* cheese, olive oil, the slightly spicy mountain honey, *torrone* nougat and other almond or walnut sweetmeats from Nuoro.

Dining Out

Traditional Sardinian cuisine has the taste of the island itself—aromatic, tangy, sometimes sharp, sometimes sweet, never dull. The flavours of the food are dictated by the wild herbs grazed in the pastures by the cattle, sheep and goats. And they say there are as many different kinds of bread as there are cheeses in France—400 at last count.

To Start With...

That bread. The best known is the *pani karasau*, twice-baked and wafer thin, so that Italian mainlanders refer to it as *carta di musica*, sheets of music. It is often served lightly salted with hot olive oil. It may also be covered with a layer of cheese, tomatoes and eggs—*pani frattau*. Otherwise, a good Sardinian meal begins with *antipasti*—melon or fresh figs with thinly sliced ham, cold vegetables marinated in olive oil and lemon or the pungent local salami. Or with pasta: *culingiones*, ravioli stuffed with cheese or spinach, sometimes flavoured with mint, and *malloreddus*, spiral *gnocchi*-like quills. The sauces are likely to be tomato or a light fresh cheese.

Fish or Meat?

Strangely enough, it is only with 20th-century tourism that Sardinia has taken to cooking fish. In the resorts, fish from local waters are served grilled, at best barbecued over charcoal: *dentici* (sea bream), *orate* (gilthead), *triglie* (mullet), *spigole* (sea bass) and *aragosta* (spiny lobster).

The great local meat speciality is suckling pig *(porcheddu)*, lamb *(agneddu)* or kid goat *(cabriddu)* roasted on a spit over an open fire and basted to give the meat a golden, crispy skin. On festive occasions, it may be served mountain-style, buried in a bed of hot embers and covered with smouldering branches of aromatic myrtle, juniper and rosemary.

Cheese and Desserts

Pecorino, the hard ewe's milk cheese, comes in two tangy varieties, *romano* and *sardo*. The favourite goat cheese is *fiore sardo*. For a gentler taste, try the *bonassai*, a mixture of ewe's and goat's milk.

Dining Out

All the flavours of the mountains mingle in Sardinia's traditional cuisine.

The famous island dessert is the *sebada*, a kind of doughnut doused in one of the myriad honeys, thick, creamy, even slightly bitter-sweet from the mountain heath blossoms or light and very sweet from orange blossom and eucalyptus. And every town produces its own variations of sweetmeats, *dolci sardi*, small almond, hazel or walnut cakes and biscuits, the best in and around Nuoro and Oliena.

Drinks

Traditionally, wine was heavy and soporific—over 15° alcohol content. Now the tastes of Italian mainlanders and modern production methods have produced more delicate and subtle wines. The best of the reds is the Cannonau from around Oliena and Dorgali and the Monica from the Campidano. These southwest vineyards also produce the time-honoured Nuragus white wine first introduced by the Romans. Other good dry whites are the Aragosta from around Alghero and the Vermentino from the northern Gallura. Dessert wines include the Malvasia and sherry-like Vernaccia. They make a mean *abbardente* or grappa from distilled myrtle, while local liqueurs may be perfumed with thyme or aniseed.

Sports

Water Sports
The swimming is good practically everywhere, with the exception of the beaches close to the industrial ports of Cagliari and Porto Torres. Wind-surfing is practised all around the island, but the winds are best on the north coast. Sailing is of course a truly royal sport on the Costa Smeralda, where you *can* rent a yacht if you don't already own one. Paragliding is becoming very popular, but water-skiing is increasingly restricted to protect swimmers.

Fishing
Underwater fishing is good at Capo Carbonara in the south, Santa Teresa Gallura in the north, as well as Bosa Marina and Alghero's Capo Caccia. Many of the ports hire out boats and crew for deepsea fishing. Freshwater anglers can try their hand on the Fiumendosa river, best as far upriver as you can go, as well as the Mannu, Cedrino and Tirso rivers and the lakes and lagoons around Oristano.

Tennis
Most major hotels have their own courts, many floodlit for cooler after-dark play, with whole clubs of them at places like Porto Cervo or Santa Margherita di Pula in the south.

Golf
Sardinia boasts two of Europe's most beautiful 18-hole courses—Pevero Golf Club, at Costa Smeralda's Cala di Volpe, and the Is Molas Golf Hotel at Santa Margherita di Pula.

Horseback Riding
Your hotel can arrange to hire a horse and the local tourist information office provides details of itineraries for the increasingly popular pastime of trekking through the Barbagia forests.

Hiking and Skiing
Tourist information offices have detailed maps for hiking in the Gennargentu, the Sopramonte or other mountain ranges. And if you find yourself in Sardinia in the winter, try the skiing up at Fonni—very good cross-country pistes.

Horse Racing
Two tracks for summer racing: Cagliari's Spiaggia del Poetto and Sassari's Rizzedu.

The Hard Facts

To plan your trip, here are some of the practical details you should know about Sardinia.

Airports
Regular international flights come into Cagliari, Alghero and Olbia, with stopovers and transfers in Milan, Rome or Naples. Summer charters ensure a direct service to all three airports. The terminals provide banking, car-hire and tourist information office services, in additon to duty-free shop, restaurant and snack bar facilities. If you do not have special bus arrangements as part of your tour package, there are taxis and airport buses to take you to most of the major resort towns.

Climate
Sardinia has a pleasant six-month summer, hot and dry from May to October. Temperatures in July and August are frequently over 30°C (86°F) and not much lower in June and September, but you can always cool off in the sea or up in the mountains. The mildest months on the coasts are May and October. Two summer winds sweep the island—the *maestrale* or mistral from the northwest and the stifling *scirocco* from the south, often bringing in sand from the Sahara. Winters may be mild on the coasts but are generally cold and rainy, with snows in the mountainous interior. April is cool and unpredictable.

Communications
The postal service in Italy is notoriously slow. But it has a modern telecommunication system for fax and phone. Call worldwide with telecards from street-phones, cheaper than the hotel's surcharge service.

Crime
No, the island is not full of bandits, nor will your children be kidnapped, but pickpockets are on the increase at the beach and in crowded places in town. Without undue paranoia, don't tempt them—very often they may be fellow tourists—with an open handbag or a wallet in the hip pocket. Leave your valuables in the hotel safe. Lock your luggage before leaving it with porters at the airport.

Customs
EC regulations apply. Customs controls are minimal at point of

entry, with an official import allowance duty-free (subject to frequent change, age limit 17) of 200 cigarettes or 40 cigars or 250 g of tobacco and 1 litre of spirits plus 2 litres still wine. A warning about drugs: be careful about importing certain prescription medicines, as these may require an official medical certificate. Import and export of local and foreign currency is limited to Lit 20,000,000.

Driving

If you are renting a car, be sure to have a valid national licence or International Driving Permit. You will find local rental firms very competitive in price with the major international companies. Rental age limit is usually over 21, sometimes over 25. Speed limits are 50 kph (31 mph) in built-up areas and 90 kph (56 mph) on the highway. Drive on the right, overtake on the left. Sardinia's drivers are fast, but generally less impatient than mainland Italians, who are here in force in the summer. Except for a few bumpy mountain roads, Sardinia's highways are in excellent condition, especially the north-south "Carlo Felice" toll-free *Superstrada* between Porto Torres and Cagliari.

Fuel is quite expensive, and many filling stations close for lunch on weekdays from 12.30 to 3 p.m., also Saturday afternoon and all day Sunday. Most filling stations only accept cash.

    Diesel   *gasolio*
    Petrol   *benzina*
    Lead-free   *senza piombo*

Emergencies

Most problems can be handled at your hotel desk. Telephone number for *carabinieri*: **112**, general emergency: **113**.

Embassies and consulates are in Rome. The UK has a Consular Office in Cagliari, but help is there only for critical situations, lost passports or worse, *not* for lost cash or plane tickets.

Formalities

A valid passport is all that most visitors will need—just an identity card for members of EC countries. No visa is required for European or North American citizens for stays of less than 3 months.

Health

Most health problems are from too much sun or midday wine. Avoid excessive direct exposure to that Mediterranean heat. Wear a hat, use a sun-screen, and keep to the shady side of the street when sightseeing. The summer heat is drier than you might imagine, so drink plenty of mineral water to avoid dehydration, even when you don't feel thirsty.

The Hard Facts

British travellers can claim health services under EC regulations. Before leaving home, obtain Form E111 from the Department of Social Security. American and Canadian tourists should check whether their medical insurance is applicable in Italy, as the regulations are frequently changing. Doctors, dentists and hospital staff are of generally good standard, many speaking some English (or German or French). If you anticipate the need for prescription medicines, take your own as you may not find the exact equivalent on the spot.

Holidays and festivals

Sardinia's public holidays are:

January 1	New Year
January 6	Epiphany
	Easter Monday (movable)
April 25	Liberation Day
May 1	Labour Day
August 15	Assumption
November 1	All Saints
December 8	Immaculate Conception
December 25	Christmas
December 26	St Stephen's Day

Religious (and pagan) festivals:

Feb.	Pre-Lenten Carnival, big in Oristano and the Barbagia, especially Mamoiada
May	1, Sant'Efisio procession, Cagliari; Penultimate Sunday, Cavalcata Sarda, Sassari
June	2, Anniversary of Garibaldi's death, Caprera
July	6–7, *Ardia* horserace for Sant'Antine, Sedilo; Equestrian events in Cagliari and Sassari
Aug.	15, Assumption procession, Orgosolo; Open-air opera in Roman amphitheatre, Cagliari; End of month, *Festa del Redentore* (Redeemer), Nuoro
Sept.	12–14, Santa Croce festival, Oristano

Languages

In addition to the Sardinian language—Catalan in Alghero—most islanders speak "regular" Italian. At the resorts, hotel and restaurant staff speak some English, German or French.

Media

British and other European newspapers and overseas editions of the *International Herald Tribune* and *Wall Street Journal* arrive on the island on the date of publication, but may take a day to reach outlying resorts. Many hotels have satellite-dish reception for BBC, CNN, German and other non-Italian TV. If you are a short-

THE HARD FACTS

wave enthusiast, find out from BBC World Service or Voice of America their current local wavelengths.

Money
The Italian unit of currency is the Lira (Lit.). Coins: 50, 100, 200 and 500 Lire. Banknotes: 1,000, 2,000, 5,000, 10,000, 50,000 and 100,000 Lire. Shops and restaurants welcome credit cards, as well as Eurocheques and traveller's cheques.

Opening hours
We give the following times as a general guide, some of them subject to variations.

Banks open Monday to Friday 8.30 to 12.45 p.m. and an hour in the afternoon.

Most *shops* are open Tuesday to Saturday from 8.30 a.m. to 12.30 p.m. and from 3.30 p.m to 8 or 8.30 p.m.

Hours for most *museums and historic sites* vary according to season and place so check with the local tourist information office. However most are closed Sunday afternoons and all day Monday.

Public Transport
Buses operated by several different companies offer a slow but pleasant way of exploring the countryside, particularly if you are organizing a walking tour. Check carefully on return times. The PANI bus line runs an express *torpedoni* service between Sassari, Nuoro and Cagliari: Sassari–Cagliari in 3 hours. Trains serve the major cities, but are slow and infrequent. The main lines are Olbia to Sassari, Olbia to Cagliari, Cagliari to Sassari. There are also branch lines and a narrow-gauge railway that links Cagliari to Arbatax, an 8-hour trip through the mountains.

Social graces
The Sardinians' time-honoured reputation for reserve and silence does not mean they are unfriendly. Their dignity is quite refreshing and their hospitality unstinting once you have struck up an acquaintance. The year-round presence of tourists has accustomed them to boisterous behaviour. They shake hands but would be disconcerted by a Latin hug. While they won't expect you to break into fluent Sardinian, they will be pleasantly surprised to hear you greet them with a couple of words of Italian. A *buon giorno* (good morning) or *buona sera* (good evening), *per piacere* (please), *grazie* (thanks) and *prego* (don't mention it) are always welcome. And however casually attired you might be for the beach or the café, remember to dress decently when entering a church.

THE HARD FACTS

Tipping
Service and VAT (IVA) are included in restaurant and hotel bills, but it's customary to tip an extra 5 or 10%, also in cafés and bars. Be careful when paying by credit card to fill in the "Total" line, often left blank for you to add, if you wish, an extra tip.

Toilets
When a little male or female figure does not indicate which is which, you should know that the women's room is usually signposted *Signore* or *Donne* and the men's by *Signori* or *Uomini*. If you are wary of public toilets, use the facilities in a bar or restaurant, but it is customary to order at least a drink there.

Tourist Information Offices
The offices run by Ente Provinciale per il Turismo (EPT) and Azienda Autonoma di Soggiorno e Turismo (AAST) are useful for museum opening hours, maps and especially mountain itineraries for hiking. In small localities, Pro Loco offices provide only local information.

Voltage
Electric current is 220-volt 50-cycle A.C., but take adaptors for any sensitive equipment like portable computers. Sockets are made for plugs with two or three pins in various shapes and arrangements; if you haven't an adaptor for your hairdryer you can easily buy a plug on the spot.

Series editor: Barbara Ender
Layout: Luc Malherbe
Photos: Zanardi, covers, pp. 4, 15, 19, 26, 29, 36, 45;
B. Joliat, pp. 22, 52, 58; Supportivisivi, pp. 10, 49
Maps: Elsner & Schichor

Copyright © 1996 by JPM Publications SA
12 avenue William-Fraisse, 1006 Lausanne, Switzerland

All rights reserved. No part of this book may be reproduced or transmitted in any form or by any means, electronic or mechanical, including photocopying, recording or by any information storage and retrieval system without permission in writing from the publisher.

Every care has been taken to verify the information in the guide, but the publisher cannot accept responsibility for any errors that may have cropped up. If you spot an inaccuracy or a serious omission, please let us know. Printed in Switzerland.